CTO IN THE
LOOP

**A Business Fable About Leading Engineers,
and Staying Human Through AI**

Copyright

Published by: Massive Paws Publishing Inc.
ISBN: 979-8-9994605-1-6

First Edition
Printed in the United States of America

Acknowledgments

A book like *CTO in the Loop* is never written alone.

It's shaped by every engineer who shipped through impossible deadlines, every PM who held the messy threads together, every designer who pushed for clarity, every leader who fought the quiet battles no one saw. Their fingerprints are everywhere in these pages.

To the teams I've been lucky enough to build with: thank you for letting me witness real craft, real courage, and real humanity. Every chapter in this book carries echoes of your grit.

To the mentors and leaders who gave me the responsibility long before I was ready: thank you for the trust that shaped me.

To Mei, Carlos, Jack, Priya, Amira, Ava and to the 100s of real people whose spirit they represent: thank you for the lessons, the conflicts, the breakthroughs, and the laughter that made the journey real.

And to my family: your patience and grounding kept me in the loop when everything else pulled me out of it.

This book is as much yours as it is mine.

Introduction

CTO in the Loop is a story about engineering leadership told from the inside - not the glossy keynote version, but the real loop: the build → break → learn → rebuild cycle that shapes every team, every system, and every leader.

It follows Sameer "Sam" Desai through twelve stages of growth - from a rainy hackathon in Portland to the hollow triumph of an IPO, to the quiet reset that forces him to ask what leadership actually means in a world racing toward automation.

This book doesn't preach frameworks. It shows how they emerge.

It doesn't romanticize startups. It reveals their emotional geometry.

And it doesn't present engineering leadership as a straight line.
It presents it as a loop - one that repeats, deepens, and reshapes you.

Underneath the narrative is a single through-line: the steel thread - the smallest, clearest end-to-end story that carries value. What begins as a product principle becomes a leadership principle... and eventually, a life principle.

My hope is that *CTO in the Loop* becomes a companion to your own journey - whether you're an engineer stepping into leadership, a founder building from chaos, or a CTO trying to keep your organization aligned with reality, not rhetoric.

Because leadership isn't an endpoint.
It's a runtime. And you learn by staying in the loop.

How to Use This Book

This isn't just a story - it's an engineering leadership interface.
Each chapter blends narrative with practical insight you can apply immediately. Here's how to read *CTO in the Loop*:

1. Read the narrative for emotional context.

The story gives shape to the messy, human moments that technical documentation usually avoids.

2. Use the Business Snapshots to anchor reality.

Stage Name, valuation, headcount, profitability, infra bill - these snapshots map Sam's journey to real startup stages.

3. Treat "Concept Learned" as your toolkit.

Every chapter decodes one engineering leadership principle:
MVP discipline, SOLID, Git hygiene, topology of teams, Conway's Law, engineering maturity, remote leadership, and more.

Make these your own or reach out for tailored advice.

4. Apply the "How Sam Applied It" patterns.

These are tactical, real-world templates from someone inside the loops - not a consultant outside them.

5. Revisit chapters when your environment changes.

The loops repeat. The lessons deepen each time you encounter them. Think of this book as a story-led operating manual for engineering leadership.

The Interface of This Book

CTO in the Loop is intentionally structured like a system diagram:

Narrative
    → **Reflection**
        → **Snapshot**
            → **Concept**
                → **Application**

This interface ensures the book works for:

- CTOs
- Engineering managers
- Founders
- Tech Leads
- High-ambition ICs
- Students stepping into systems for the first time
- Anyone navigating scale, uncertainty, or complexity

You won't need to know every acronym to understand the lessons.
But if you've lived through production outages, roadmap churn, scaling pains, mergers, layoffs, compliance waves, or IPO theatrics - you'll feel at home here.

This book gives language to the things engineering leaders experience but rarely articulate.

Author's Note

CTO in the Loop is a fictionalized narrative built from real experiences across startups, scale-ups, enterprise turnarounds, and AI-era transformations. The characters, companies, and events are composites created to tell emotional truths cleanly and safely.

It is not a biography.
It is a synthesis: of people, patterns, and decisions that repeat across organizations.

If you've led teams, you'll recognize the loops.
If you're stepping into leadership, this book will help you anticipate them.

This book is my attempt to document what shapes engineering leaders: the small decisions, the invisible debts, the quiet courage, and the clarity earned through exhaustion, not enthusiasm.

Leadership is a refactor. This book is one version of mine.

Dedication

- To the builders who ship through uncertainty.
- To the leaders who stay human in systems that forget humanity.
- To the mentors who rewired my loops.
- To my family, you're the only architecture that has always scaled gracefully.

Table of Contents

Chapter 1

The Weekend That Changed Everything

The drizzle wasn't rain so much as a mist, the kind that settled on your hoodie and slowly crept into your bones before you realized you were wet. Most Portland evenings have a way of blurring the line between air and water. Sameer "Sam" Desai hunched against the damp, jogging the last block toward the coworking space. His glasses had fogged twice already; he wiped them with his sleeve, leaving streaks that blurred the neon-lit street.

He muttered under his breath: "Startup Weekend. Let's see if you're worth the free pizza."

His roommate's voice echoed in his head: *Startup Weekend? Isn't that just speed-dating for nerds?*

Sam had smirked at that. "Exactly. Worst case, I waste two days. Best case, I get to build something instead of patching someone else's suboptimal C# code"

That was the truth: boredom. His job - maintaining custom-built online banking sites for a mid-size SaaS company - paid the bills, but every sprint felt like duct-taping leaky pipes. Tonight was a chance, however slim, to do something different.

He pulled the coworking door open and promptly stepped into chaos.

The space buzzed like a beehive.

150+ strangers milled in clusters, some arguing animatedly, others furiously scribbling on Post-its. Whiteboards leaned against every wall, covered in half-legible diagrams of arrows, clouds, and boxes. The air smelled of permanent markers, reheated pizza, and too much ambition. Someone had dragged a couch into a corner, already occupied by two people hunched over laptops like monks at a shrine.

Sam stopped at the doorway, taking it all in. His nervous energy was palpable. Some people were clearly students, wide-eyed and eager. Others had the confident weariness of tech professionals as if lightning could strike again. A few wore suits, which looked almost indecent among the hoodies, jeans and shorts.

The organizer whistled loudly into the microphone for attention. "Okay everyone! Time to pitch! Ninety seconds each. Convince people to join you, and the top 10 popular ideas get to form teams and build their product by Sunday night."

Sam hadn't planned to pitch. He figured he'd float into a group, write some backend code, and leave Sunday night with a few new local connections. But as he listened, his patience thinned.

A man in a tie pitched a dating site for dogs and cats. A woman in bright big glasses pitched a scalable "kissing booth". Another pitched the newest ayurvedic formulation for hair regrowth. Sam snorted into his sleeve. *Somewhere, Darwin is shaking his head.*

And then something shifted in him. He'd been stewing for months, watching his younger cousins stress over careers after college - too many options, not enough guidance. He had sketched an idea in a notebook once, left it to gather dust. Now, almost without thinking, his hand went up.

An Unplanned Pitch

"Hi, I'm Sam," he began, his voice steadier than he expected.

"I've been watching young people - especially college students - get paralyzed by career choices. Too many options, no guidance, endless stress. I want to build an app that makes exploration feel like a journey, not a panic attack."

He saw a few heads turn and nod in agreement. Encouraging.

"Upload a résumé, connect your LinkedIn profile, answer a few questions, and the app shows real career paths others have taken - patterns, trajectories, possibilities. Not surgical and specific answers, just data-driven guidance. Think of it as a GPS for your next stop in the journey."

He hesitated, then added: "We'll call it CareerLens."

He stepped back, heart pounding. The room buzzed with whispers. Someone scribbled notes.

The volunteer host nodded. "Thank you, Sam."

Sam exhaled, surprised by the adrenaline rushing through him. *Well, now my idea is out there. Let's see if anyone cares.*

They did. His idea was the 4th most popular by votes!

Within the hour, a small team coalesced around him.

First came Carlos Rivera, tall, magnetic, with a grin that suggested he was born ready to pitch and sell. He declared himself "business side" without being asked, already promising to "handle the judges."

Next was Mei Chen, the woman who had been sketching during other pitches. She introduced herself quietly, then slid a napkin toward him. On it were wireframes of a career questionnaire and a dashboard. Clean, precise, practical.

"You pitched. I sketched. This can work," she said.

By midnight, there were more stragglers: a young marketer who claimed she could make anything go viral but fell asleep under a desk, and a college kid who coded frantically before disappearing Sunday morning. But the core was set: Sam, Carlos, and Mei.

Sam took charge without trying.

He spun up a GitHub repository.
He set up a shared google drive.
And taped some Post-its to a makeshift Kanban board: *To Do, Doing, Done.*

Carlos roamed the room, pitching CareerLens to anyone within earshot. "We'll disrupt career guidance! We'll dethrone LinkedIn in 12 months!"

Mei refined her sketches, moving from napkin to laptop with surgical focus.

At one point, Mei asked, "Blue button or green button?"

Sam shook his head. "Neither. Not yet."

He drew on the whiteboard: a stick figure labeled *Student* on the left, another labeled *Actionable Career Advice* on the right, and a single line connecting them.

"This is our steel thread," he explained. "Not the whole bridge, just one cable across the canyon. If it holds, we know we can build the rest. If it snaps, at least we fail and learn early."

Carlos frowned. "We need features. Dashboards. Maybe remote video coaching."

"One cable," Sam repeated. "Log in, upload résumé, get advice. That's the end-to-end story. If we nail that, we're alive."

Mei finally looked up. "One cable. One story. I like it."

Carlos sighed. "Fine. But if we lose because we don't have video coaching, it will all be on you!"

Sam smirked. *If we lose, it won't be because we skipped video coaching.*

36 very blurry hours

Sam hunched over his laptop, piecing together their "backend" with free Microsoft Azure credits and duct-taped scripts. Mei translated sketches into clickable mock-ups. Carlos rehearsed in hallways, occasionally barging in with, "Ready yet?"

Sam almost spit out his soda when he checked the time. 3 a.m.!

Mei was explaining CSS to Carlos. "This button? Not just blue. hex #007BFF. Write it down."

Carlos dutifully scribbled it into his notebook like it was scripture.

Other teams floundered. One fought over whether their app should be called *Pawfect* or *PetPal*. Another deleted their entire code by accident. By comparison, CareerLens looked inappropriately professional.

Still, the stress showed. At one point their database crashed, and Sam spent an hour muttering prayers into Stack Overflow. Carlos overwrote Mei's mock-ups in the repo and nearly got banned from touching his own laptop. Mei introduced Sam to bubble tea, insisting it was "designer fuel." He almost choked on the tapioca balls but eventually fell in love with the flavor.

Through it all, the steel thread held.

Sunday afternoon arrived way too soon.

As their demo loomed, the team rehearsed many times. The first time, the résumé upload feature crashed. The second time, their advice engine spit out gibberish.

"Third time is the charm," Sam muttered, as he pushed the latest version of the backend.

An unexpected outcome

The lights dimmed for the final pitches. Judges leaned forward, pens ready.

Carlos strode onto the stage with practiced confidence. "CareerLens is the compass for your future. Upload your résumé, and we show you successful paths others have walked - real data, relatable journeys, concrete advice."

He clicked through Mei's slides: clean, and, compelling. Then came the moment of truth.

Login. Résumé upload. Career advice output.

It worked.

The judges leaned in. One whispered to another. Someone clapped early.

When the winners were announced, Sam barely heard.

"First place... CareerLens!"

Carlos whooped, hugging strangers. Mei smiled for the first time all weekend. Sam stood frozen, hands in his pockets, stunned at the weight of applause.

They had won.

After the crowd dispersed, pizza boxes stacked like monuments to survival, Sam lingered at their table. Mei packed her laptop. Carlos disappeared to celebrate. Sam sat alone, staring at the whiteboard where their steel thread still hung in marker strokes.

One cable. End-to-end. Enough to carry them across.

For the first time in years, he savored the messy joy of creation - not as a cog, not as a maintainer, but as a builder.

He wasn't a founder chasing investors. He wasn't a suit selling buzzwords.

But he was the one who stretched the cable across the canyon. And it held.

On his walk home, drizzle soaking his hoodie again, he thought: *Chaos isn't the problem. Chaos is the point.*

Closing Business Snapshot

Stage	Prototype
Company Value	$0
ARR	$0
Annual Profit	Negative $85 (Pizza & doughnut Debt)
Funding Raised	$0
Total Employees	0 (just Weekend Volunteers)
Engineering Employees	0 (Sam + Mei for now)
Sam's Equity	0%
Infra Bill	$0 (Free Cloud Credits)

Concept Learned: Minimum Viable Product

Sam learned early that progress in a startup isn't measured by scope, design, or lines of code - it's measured by proof. He called it the MVP aka "steel thread," the thinnest possible working version that could carry the full weight of an idea. The MVP was that thread made real. It wasn't a prototype for show or a presentation slide that implied potential. It was the simplest, working path that tied users' needs to outcome.

At the hackathon, every team claimed they were building something "game changing." Most got stuck in debate - what tech stack, what feature set, what edge case. Sam's team barely agreed on a name. But when he reframed the goal - *"one story that actually runs end-to-end"* - the confusion cleared. The MVP became a focusing mechanism. Instead of "building a platform," they built evidence. That mindset would later shape how Sam evaluated everything - features, processes, even leadership decisions. If it doesn't produce a measurable signal of value, it's just noise.

How Sam Realized the MVP concept

Sam reduced the problem to a single user journey: login → résumé upload → 5 pieces of actionable career advice. He called it the "proof path." Each step had to work, not perfectly, but completely. The team wanted dashboards, metrics, and animations. Sam kept asking, "Does this help the thread hold?" When they hit time pressure, those constraints saved them. They cut the extras and concentrated on function.

On demo day, the judges didn't see polish - they saw completion. The app accepted input, processed data, and produced feedback. The system held. It was fragile but alive. That was enough. The MVP didn't win because it was beautiful; it won because it worked. And that single win taught Sam his first leadership habit: simplify until the outcome speaks for itself.

Chapter 2

The First Refactor

The café downstairs always smelled like burnt beans.

Every morning when Sam pushed open the heavy glass door to the second-floor sublet, the aroma hit him first; only then did the room snap into focus - three mismatched Ikea desks; a fourth desk, a former breakfast table donated by Mei's parents; a whiteboard so saturated with Expo ink that faint ghosts of old diagrams haunted every new sketch; a heater that clicked, wheezed, and then rattled like a box of bolts. The ceiling fans didn't rotate so much as gesture at the idea.

Six months earlier, CareerLens had won the hackathon and made them minor celebrities for exactly a week and a half. Winning felt like holding lightning in the hand. Building afterward felt like standing in a storm with a metal rod and calling that "a plan."

Within 3 months, they had scraped together a $100,000 seed check from a few local angels - just enough for used furniture, two MacBooks on payment plans, and ramen-level salaries always paid out a week too late. Suddenly, it was real. Not glamorous. Not secure. Just in-your-face real.

Sam - still technically "Engineer" on paper - had self-appointed as CEO because somebody had to take investor calls and sign the sublease. He hated the title. It sounded like performative theater. Most days, his job was the least CEO-like thing you could imagine: debugging race conditions with a space heater roaring like a jet engine two feet from his chair.

"Morning," Mei said from behind dual monitors, a cup of tea steaming beside her trackpad. She had been there before him.... again. "Coffee downstairs smells like burnt popcorn. Do not even try."

"I already made the mistake," Sam said, holding up the paper cup like a cautionary sign. "This is more of an engineer's prop than a beverage."

On the third desk sat Carlos, thumbing through his pitch notebook, redlining phrases as if he were editing scripture.

He didn't look up. "Good, you're here. We need to hire three engineers by Christmas."

Sam set down his bag. "Today is October 20th"

"Exactly," Carlos said, as if time itself were negotiable. "Investors want velocity. Velocity comes from headcount."

Mei didn't glance away from her online canvas. "We have barely onboarded one engineer so far, let alone three."

The heater coughed. The espresso grinder downstairs screamed like someone blending nails.

At that exact moment Jack Porter pushed open the door - a laconic, wry senior engineer Sam had coaxed from his network with promises of interesting problems and a chair that wasn't broken. Jack surveyed the room, took in the whiteboard full of arrows pointing at angrier arrows, and dropped his backpack with a thud.

"Quick status check," Jack said. "Are we still committing straight to main like a demolition derby? Because if so, adding three more cowboys just gives us a parade."

Carlos bristled. "We need to move."

"We don't need to set our server on fire," Mei said.

Sam rubbed the bridge of his nose. He was both the person who kept the product alive and the person expected to sell a bright future. The job titles on their nonexistent org chart were a joke. What they had were infinite problems, and a steel thread stretched across them.

"Okay," he said, palms open like a referee. "We're going to do two things today. One: create a realistic backlog. Two: stop pushing to production like we're parked on the Autobahn."

Carlos stared. "But the demo...."

"The demo will work better if we don't deploy half-baked changes while you're mid-sentence," Sam said. "Ask me how I know."

He knew because last week, during a practice pitch to an investor, the app crashed so hard the only thing left was the 500 error's blinking cursor, like a heartbeat flatlining in public.

Jack slid into the chair opposite Sam. "I vote we also buy a new space heater before this one eats a bird."

"Third priority," Sam said. "Right after branch protection rules and maybe some sanity."

Roadmap Day: Evolving Chaos into a Plan

They tore sticky notes into smaller sticky notes and built their first official backlog. It looked like an archaeological dig: layers of hacks from the hackathon weekend; a sediment of TODOs; an occasional sparkly feature request that had no business being there but was too pretty to throw away.

"Brand new feature requests don't go in 'Prioritized,'" Mei said, plucking a neon note from Carlos's hand and dropping it into "Someday/Maybe."

Carlos sighed dramatically. "Investors love maps and dashboards."

"Users love things that don't break," Jack muttered.

They argued about prioritization: Should they refactor the recommendation engine before courting more users, or chase two contracts that Carlos said were "warm" (which meant the prospects had once nodded at him in a hallway)? Mei wanted to solidify onboarding; Jack wanted to pay down tech debt; Carlos wanted glossy graphs; Sam wanted a nap and a second brain.

In the end, Sam compromised with a stack-ranked, limited "Now" column: three items max, no exceptions.

"Three?" Carlos said, scandalized.

"Three," Sam said. "That's already one more than any good team can truly juggle."

He wrote the first three on the whiteboard in firm strokes:

1. Stabilize upload + parsing: no more mysterious file-type errors.
2. Instrument the advice engine: observability, not guesses.
3. Build a sandbox demo environment: no demoing against prod again, ever.

"Look at that," Jack said. "A plan that fits on a sticky note, which is also the unit of time we have left to live."

Sam grinned despite himself.

Process, or Something Like It: Aka Bare-Minimum Rituals

Stand-up the next morning was a caricature: Sam on time, Mei three minutes early, Jack five minutes late by design, Carlos broadcasting from a cab with his phone at chin level like a tourist in an exotic locale.

"Today's goal is simple," Sam said. "We introduce pull requests. No more pushing straight to production."

Jack raised a hand. "I propose we tattoo that on Carlos's forearm."

Carlos's cab hit a pothole hard enough that the phone went sideways. "Very funny."

Sam continued, "Branch protection rules are on. CI must pass to merge. We'll do code reviews - short, frequent, kind."

"Define 'kind,'" Jack said.

"Less than 3 sentences of sarcasm."

"That's cruel."

They tried to do a standup again the next day, and half the team simply forgot. On day three, Sam set a timer, posted an agenda, and kept them under ten minutes. He was discovering a law of startups that none of his engineering books had explained: habits only become culture when you continue them even on the worst of days and the best of days.

Branch Protection Meets Reality

It didn't take long for the new branch protections to collide with the old chaos. That afternoon, the app started throwing 500s again. Jack triaged, Mei tested, and Sam tailed logs like a gambler staring at a slot machine.

"Who merged without review?" Jack asked.

A quiet hand went up at the door - their part-time front-end dev, who had started strong and then faded like a bad chorus.

"It was a trivial change," the dev said. "I'm sorry."

Jack inhaled, about to launch into a speech. Sam lifted a palm. "Okay. No blame. But this is why reviews exist. Two pairs of eyes save us public facepalms"

He wanted to be angry, and he wasn't. He was scared. That was worse. Funding could survive a bad sprint; it couldn't survive the reputation of a team that treated production like a sketchpad.

He spent the evening pair-programming with the dev, wrote a merge checklist that fit on a sticky note, and scheduled a Friday learning hour titled "Drama-free deployments." Jack drew him a poster: a cowboy on a horse labeled "main," riding into a cactus.

They taped both works of art by the door.

The Lunch Whiteboard

On Thursday, Sam commandeered the whiteboard while he ordered noodles from the place that sent chopsticks the thickness of pencils.

"All right," he said to the team. "I'm going to channel my inner professor for ten minutes. It's either this, or we keep playing whack-a-bug with our future."

Jack slumped theatrically. "Class is in session."

"**SOLID principles**," Sam wrote. "Not a religion. Guardrails."

- **S - Single Responsibility.** "Don't make one person cook, serve, *and* wash dishes. They'll burn out. Code is the same. One purpose per module. If a function is doing three different jobs, we've created a tired line cook."
- **O - Open/Closed.** "Open to extension, closed to modification. Think **Lego**. Don't keep re-carving the same block; click on a new one. Feature flags help us add without ripping out plumbing."
- **L - Liskov Substitution.** "If I hand you a plug adaptor, you expect anything that says 'plug' to behave like a plug. In code: subclasses should not surprise the base type. Surprises belong in birthdays, not in interfaces."
- **I - Interface Segregation.** "Don't hand a diner a phone book when they just want to order noodles. Give small, focused menus. Small interfaces mean fewer accidental commitments."
- **D - Dependency Inversion.** "High-level policy shouldn't depend on the low-level nuts and bolts. We decide *what* we want first, then decide *how* we do it. It's like writing the recipe before buying the specific pan."

Mei nodded. "So our 'super component' that does routing, state, and UI is... a tired line cook?"

"A heroic, exhausted, spaghetti-covered master chef," Sam clarified.

Jack smirked. "Lego > spaghetti. Accepted."

"Hold your applause," Sam said, grinning. "We'll check in on how this actually changes our confidence next week."

First Remote Experiment

That afternoon, they welcomed Priya Nair, a product manager Sam had met at a meetup, joining part-time and remote from Seattle. She was polished, curious and asked the kind of questions that immediately revealed where your thinking had gaps.

Their first video call froze on her mid-blink. At one point, her audio lagged five seconds behind, so Sam's question and Priya's answer did a kind of long-distance duet.

"Pretend this is intentional," Jack whispered. "We've invented asynchronous product management."

They laughed, but Sam's brain was already filing this under "inevitable future." If CareerLens worked, there would not be five people in one room forever. The sooner they learned to hum while remote, the less likely the engine would stall when the car sped up.

Priya followed up the disastrous call with a beautifully written google doc outlining onboarding goals, user interview scripts, and risks. She included a small section titled "We owe users clarity more than features." Sam became an instant fan of Priya after reading that doc.

When Intent Alone Isn't Enough

Two weeks later, Sam took a walk with the part-time front-end dev - the one who hadn't just merged without review but had also rewritten the main branch's history at 1:17 a.m. - erasing the audit trail - disabled the failing CI test step, and hard-coded a live API key to "get it green." When the build polluted logs with customer emails, he tried to rewrite history instead of paging the team.

They circled the block around the café while Sam rehearsed and then abandoned the rehearsal entirely.

"You're talented," Sam said. "But last night wasn't a mistake. There were three choices: bypassing the process, exposing data, and hiding it. We talked about this after the first incident. I can't run a team on luck."

The dev stared at the sidewalk. "I was trying to unblock the launch."

"I get the intent," Sam said. "Intent doesn't protect customers. Integrity does."

Silence for half a block.

"I'll pay you for the month," Sam said. "If anyone calls, I'll be honest: your UI work was solid, but I can't vouch for your judgment around production and data. That's the job."

The dev nodded once. "I knew it."

Nine minutes, two thanks, and a handshake later, it was done. A bus pulled up and exhaled like a tired animal; the dev stepped on and vanished into its belly.

Sam climbed the stairs, feeling like he'd swallowed gravel.

Firing wasn't cruel. It was clarity. It still hurt.

Mei met his eyes when he came in. She didn't say anything. She didn't have to.

The Fateful Investor Call

Their angel - Rita - was patient, but allergic to fluff. On their monthly call, she asked sensible questions no pitch deck could dodge.

"Your burn is tracking a bit high," Rita said. "What gets you to $50K ARR this quarter?"

Carlos started to respond with a story about the pipeline and warm intros. Rita held up a hand. "Not pipeline. Cash."

Sam pulled up the spreadsheet he'd massaged at midnight, fingers still ink-stained from the whiteboard marker. He walked Rita through real commitments: a small college's pilot; a guidance counselor network; two customers that were paying in "gift cards and goodwill" (he did not use that exact phrase though).

After the call, Carlos muttered, "She could smile more."

"She did," Sam said. "Right when the conversation got honest."

That night, Sam quietly skipped his stipend, pushing their runway out by three weeks. He told no one. Leadership, he was learning, sometimes meant pretending you weren't bleeding so everyone else could keep their hands steady.

A Comedy of Errors (Lightning Talk #1)

The coworking space hosted a Friday Lightning Night - five-minute talks, no slides, mostly founders telling rehearsed origin stories with dramatic pauses. Somehow, Sam got talked into giving one titled "Lessons from Our Error Logs." Mei dared him. Jack lobbied for a live crash.

Sam's talk was half confession, half stand-up.

"We met our first investor," he began, "by confidently demoing on my local dev environment and discovering, live, that our 'Forgot Password' form forgot what a password was. The lesson? Demo against a stable sandbox, not your hopes and dreams."

Laughter. He relaxed.

He told the story of branch protections and the cowboy poster by the door. He described the smell of burnt beans as their pre-deploy canary. He closed with the steel thread metaphor and the line he'd started to believe: "The chaos wasn't failure; it was the canvas. The job is to braid that chaos."

Afterward, three people asked if they were hiring. One offered to loan them a better heater.

Sam walked home in the drizzle, feeling like he'd just done stand-up in a room where the punchlines were decisions keeping a company alive.

The Tuesday Hack Night

On a wet Tuesday the following week, the coworking community hosted a hack night. Sam almost skipped; he was drowning in backlog. Mei dragged him anyway. "You need new oxygen," she said.

They sat at a table with strangers: a statistics PhD student who understood clustering better than social etiquette, a former teacher who wanted to help students pivot careers, and a barista from the downstairs coffee shop who turned out to be a Postgres whisperer.

For three hours, they prototyped a better way to explain CareerLens recommendations - not just "go be a data analyst" but "people like you moved from X to Y after learning Z." Mei sketched a tiny "Because" box under each suggestion. The student wired up a toy k-nearest neighbors' demo. The barista optimized a query so effectively that Sam wanted to offer him a job on the spot.

"That's the first thing in a week that felt like forward motion," Sam confessed to Mei as they packed up.

"That's because it wasn't just faster," she said. "It was clearer."

Sam wrote "Clarity > kindness" on a sticky note and stuck it to his monitor.

The Work Nobody Sees but Everyone Feels

At 11:40 p.m., alone in the office except for the heater's breathing and the café's dishwasher yawning below, Sam stared at the roadmap. It was still a battlefield: features fighting bugs, bugs fighting experiments, experiments fighting memos. But something had shifted. The sticky notes fit cleaner. The "Now" column had teeth. "Someday" stopped pretending to be "This afternoon."

He worked down a short checklist:

- Enable branch protections on the main repo (again - someone had manually disabled them).
- Add a pull request template that asks the three questions he kept asking out loud: "What changed? How can I test it? What am I ignoring/deferring?"
- Wire up a basic CI pipeline that runs tests and linting, then refuses to merge if either flinched.
- Write a one-pager on code review etiquette: assume good intent, comment on code, not people, praise clean abstractions, leave at least one "nit: nice" note per PR because kindness is contagious.

He broadcast to everyone on HipChat: "Tomorrow: no new features until the upload parser is boringly reliable"

He closed the laptop, let silence fill the room, and studied the whiteboard one more time. The arrows were still angling in conflicting directions, but the steel thread he'd drawn months ago had now become two:

1. upload → parse → suggest;
2. demo → sandbox → breathe.

"I founded this company by accident," he said into the empty air. "And if I don't lead, it dies."

Saying it out loud made the floor tilt and then settle. He rubbed his face, grabbed his prop coffee cup, and turned off the light. The café grinder screamed one last time like a goodnight joke.

Closing Business Snapshot

Stage	Foundation
Company Value	$500K
ARR	$50k
Annualized Profit	Negative $20k
Funding Raised	$100k
Total # Employees	10
Eng Employees	6
Sam's Equity	40% (Unvested)
Infra Bill	$400/month

Concept Learned: SOLID Principles + Git Discipline

As CareerLens gained real users, every line of code became a liability. What once felt like creativity started to feel like fragility. Sam saw stress rising - not from workload, but from uncertainty. Every change carried invisible risk.

He decided to install structure, not as control, but as alignment and compassion. SOLID principles provided mental order; Git discipline provided behavioral order. Together, they turned chaos into consistency and predictability.

In plain language, Sam explained SOLID like this: "Code should behave like a good team - each part doing one job well, designed to work together without friction." The Git rules - branch protection, reviews, CI - were the social contract version of that same idea. They didn't slow anyone down; they made collaboration safer and joyful.

How Sam Personified SOLID & Git Discipline

He made small, visible moves. He protected the main branch, enforced pull requests, and set review norms emphasizing clarity and kindness. He gave a short talk on SOLID, translating abstract acronyms into everyday metaphors: pans, Legos, and kitchens. The laughter helped it stick.

Then came the demo: Sam refactored one high-traffic module following the first two SOLID principles. The difference was immediate - fewer merge conflicts, clearer ownership, less confusion. He added a basic CI step to run tests and linters automatically. It failed often at first, but each failure taught them how to prevent the next.

Finally, he banned "live demos in dev"; instead, they built a lightweight sandbox for demos and QA.

The results became tangible within weeks: fewer 500s, smoother deploys, and calmer engineers. The product hadn't fully stabilized; but the culture had. Sam learned that discipline wasn't rigidity, it was respect. And the best engineers weren't always fast, but they were the ones who made reliability feel normal.

Chapter 3

Exit, and the Space It Opens

It had been nearly two years since that Startup Weekend.

A long time since the applause, since the adrenaline of winning first place, since Sam walked home through the Portland drizzle believing he'd finally touched something like destiny.

Now, the thrill was gone. Sameer "Sam" Desai was exhausted. The same drizzle fell outside, but he no longer felt taller in it. He felt hunched, worn down, like one of those neon signs outside the café downstairs - still glowing, but flickering at the edges.

CareerLens was still alive. Technically. "Alive" meant payroll barely met, servers limping, and morale thin as tracing paper.

When Building Feels Like Bracing

Their office had expanded from three desks to fifteen, but it felt smaller. The café's burnt coffee smell still seeped up the stairs, now competing with the odor of sweaty chairs and instant ramen. Whiteboards lined the walls, but they were cluttered with arrows, circles, sticky notes, and questions no one wanted to answer.

Carlos had become a traveling salesman in all but name. He pitched almost every week: colleges, nonprofits, training boards, anyone who would listen. He came back either glowing, "They're practically ready to sign!" or furious, "They don't get innovation!" There was rarely anything in-between.

Mei had grown quieter. Once she showcased her UX ideas with joy; now her days blurred into triage, tweaking designs to patch broken flows, and trying to keep user experience coherent. Her notebook was no longer filled with crisp diagrams. Instead it was a battlefield of crossed-out drafts.

And Sam? He was everywhere. Debugging memory leaks one hour, explaining pull requests the next, soothing a panicked investor in the afternoon, fixing a cron job at midnight. His life was Azure dashboards, a backlog of 800 emails, and a creeping sense that the company was less a rocket and more a leaky canoe.

Steel Threads in Slow Scale

In the early days, Sam had described their product as a steel cable stretched across a canyon. 18 months later, the cable was still there - but frayed, sagging, threatening to snap.

- **Engineering Roadmap:** Every meeting was split into two camps: "refactor everything before it collapses" versus "ship faster before customers leave." Nobody ever really won; they just moved the argument to the next meeting.
- **Tech Stack:** The MVP shortcuts had hardened into brittle landmines. A single change in one module could cascade into failures three systems away.
- **Processes:** Retros were supposed to be constructive. Instead they became anti-therapy. "What went well?" - Dead silence. "What didn't?" - sighs & *"Everything"* sticky notes.
- **People:** The team had grown to fifteen, but churned constantly. One engineer quit after three months, another ghosted after a fight with Carlos, a third admitted they "didn't know what the point of the product was." Morale sagged.

Jack, with his trademark sarcasm, summed it up: "We're not a startup. We're a stopgap."

Vignettes from the trenches

The Demo Disaster
Carlos had promised a community college dean that CareerLens could handle 500 concurrent users. Sam begged him not to demo live. Yet, Carlos ignored him.

After 47 students registered live and started exploring at once, the system collapsed. The dean watched error messages pile up like confetti. Carlos smiled nervously and said, "We're... stress-testing." Sam killed the server and restored the database from a backup, cheeks burning.

Oh, and the dean never called back.

The Onboarding Farce
They hired a new CS graduate, bright-eyed and eager. Day one: no company email, no laptop. Day five: no clear assignment. On day ten, he asked, "Do we have a handbook?" Jack deadpanned: "Yes. Rule 1: Duck when prod explodes." The grad quit that same Friday.

The Retro Breakdown
One retrospective, Mei scribbled on a sticky note: *"I don't know why I'm still here."* The note sat on the board for a full minute before Sam quietly moved it aside. Nobody spoke.

That silence haunted him more than the outages.

One Node Lights Up a Cluster

Amidst the chaos, one bright spot emerged: a midsize outplacement consultancy.

Unlike other clients who dabbled, they *devoured* CareerLens. Daily. Enthusiastically. They integrated it into their workflows, encouraged their advisors to depend on it, and even called out bugs politely instead of threatening to cancel.

Sam noticed it first in the logs. "They're not just testing," he told the team. "They're embedding us."

When the consultancy's CEO invited them to a meeting, Sam hoped for expansion. Instead, she leaned across the table and said:

"We don't want equity. We don't want to invest. We want your technology."

Sam froze. "You mean... acquisition?"

"Yes. The code, the IP, maybe some of the team. We'll pay cash. It makes more sense to fold CareerLens into our portfolio rather than keep paying licenses."

Sam's pulse quickened. *This is an exit. A real one. Proof we built something valuable.*

The Fork No One Planned

The news hit the team like a thunderclap.

Carlos exploded. "2+ years of sweat, nights on Azure, pitching until my throat bled - and it ends with a check from one customer? That's not an exit, that's a shameful surrender."

"It's survival," Sam said, trying to stay calm. "We repay investors. We stop bleeding cash."

Carlos paced like a caged animal. "We promised a unicorn. IPO. Vision. This is a yard sale."

Mei, always the pragmatist, closed her notebook. "Better a yard sale than a funeral. At least the product will live."

Her words landed heavier than any argument Sam could make.

A Graceful Transition

There was no fanfare. No champagne. No TechCrunch headlines. Just PDF contracts, weary lawyers, and Zoom calls where everyone kept their cameras off.

- **The offer:** $500,000 all-cash.
- **The allocation:** Enough to repay investors their $100,000 seed, with leftovers split among the founders and a small token bonus pool to employees.
- **The transition:** Mei would join the acquiring firm to keep continuity.
- **The emotions:** muted relief, not joy.

Carlos sulked through the process. His diluted share barely covered a few months' rent. "I could've made 10x more consulting," he muttered.

Mei accepted her new role with quiet grace. "At least I'll get to see the product used."

Sam received his payout - around $40,000 after taxes. He stared at the number on his banking app. Not wealth. Not glory. But closure.

Leaving With the Lesson Still Running

Relief was the first emotion that surprised him. Not triumph. Not regret. Just relief - quiet, steady, almost therapeutic.

He realized he didn't miss the investor updates or the performative urgency of board meetings. He didn't miss dressing numbers in their Sunday best for people who never touched the product. And he certainly didn't miss waking up each morning already behind.

What he *did* miss were the small, tangible joys: sketching a cleaner flow on a whiteboard, unblocking a junior, watching a test suite run green after days of red. He missed that unmistakable hum of building - what he privately called the tofu-making of startups. The unglamorous, daily, slow craft of turning raw ingredients into something that fed people.

He realized something essential about himself: he was not made for the dining room, where founders pitched visions between courses. He was made for the kitchen - steam-filled, sleeves rolled up, hands moving with purpose.

Next time, he told himself, he'd still join early. But not as a founder betting the whole house. As a builder with agency, not ownership of every burden. He didn't need the crown. He needed the craft.

On his last day, he swiped his badge and the reader blinked red. Deactivated. Of course. He stood outside the co-working space for a moment, listening to the muffled thrum inside - keyboards clicking, chairs rolling, someone laughing at a joke he would never hear the punchline to.

Strangely, the sound comforted him. Life inside was continuing. And so was his.

He slipped the dead badge into his pocket, texted a friend - "Know anyone hiring founding engineers? I've got scars and stories."

Then he stepped into the starry Portland night. No fanfare, no ceremony. Just a long exhale he hadn't realized he'd been holding, and a freedom that felt earned, not given.

The lesson didn't end when he walked away.
It came with him, still running in the background - quiet, steady, waiting to be used again.

Closing Business Snapshot

Stage	Post-Exit, Year 2
Exit	$500,000 (Asset Sale)
ARR	$200k
Annual Profit	- $180k
Funding Raised	$100k
Total Employees	15
Eng Employees	8
Sam's Payout	$35k
Infra Bill	$800/month

Concept Learned: Technical Debt vs. Emotional Debt

Sam learned that not all debt shows up on a balance sheet.
The company's codebase had grown brittle, patched, and over-extended; so had the people writing it. He began to see a pattern: every hack in the code had an emotional twin in behavior. The late-night shortcuts, the skipped retros, the silent resentments - all accumulated interest.

Technical debt was the mess you could measure. Emotional debt was the quiet exhaustion no metric captured.

Each shortcut bought time today by stealing trust from tomorrow.

In the final months before the acquisition, Sam saw both kinds of debt converge. The backlog was full of brittle logic; the chat channels were full of brittle conversations. The code still ran, but the team didn't.

He realized that cleanup wasn't just refactoring files; it was restoring honesty.

Technical debt slows a system. Emotional debt slows the entire org.

Both compound until the next release - or at least until someone decides to pay interest with courage.

How Sam Load Balanced The "Paradox of Debts"

When the buyer's due-diligence checklist arrived, Sam treated it like therapy.

He cleaned up function calls and log files with the same care he used when apologizing to teammates he'd snapped at during sprints. He refactored the fragile authentication service - the one everyone feared touching.... not because the buyer demanded it, but because it symbolized unfinished business.

He wrote a list titled "Debts to Close".

Half of it was technical: remove deprecated API calls, archive unused tables, tag endpoints consistently. The other half was human: return borrowed favors, thank Mei for her patience, acknowledge Carlos's grind even when it grated.

By the time the company handover was done, the systems were cleaner and the team lighter. He'd paid down more than technical debt; he'd cleared the emotional ledger that followed every founder too long into the next chapter.

Walking out of the coworking space for the last time, he realized closure wasn't about code reviews or contracts.
It was about debt forgiveness - given and received.

That understanding became his new principle for every future project:

Ship features fast but never let integrity accrue too much interest.

Chapter 4

Almost Scaling (On Purpose This Time)

The relief hit Sam the moment he walked through the glass doors of his new employer.

No investors in the lobby waiting for updates. No board slides to polish before stand-up. No burden of being "the founder." This time, he wasn't carrying anyone's expectations but his own.

He was simply "employee #5".

He carried a laptop, a backpack, and a quiet hunger. That was enough. No speeches. No fundraising decks. Just work.

The office itself looked like it had been furnished by a scavenger hunt: three mismatched desks from Craigslist, two rolling chairs that squeaked, and a kitchen table turned into a conference table. The walls were covered in half-erased marker doodles, as if the whiteboards were dreaming in fragments. A faint smell of new carpet mixed with yesterday's curry takeout.

For Sam, it smelled like freedom.

New Faces, Same Old Friction

Priya Nair was there, full-time now.

She had been a disembodied face on Zoom calls at his first startup, but here she was in the flesh, sticky notes in hand, pushing tasks across columns with a force that could rival gravity.

Sam felt her scrutiny before she spoke. On his first morning, he drew an architecture sketch to show how their data pipeline would evolve.

Priya tapped the corner of the diagram.

"You can't just say it *scales*. Show me the tradeoffs."

Sam bristled. "I just did."

"No. You showed arrows. I want choices."

The room stilled.

It was the first of many clashes. Beneath the sparks was something Sam respected: she demanded evidence, not content with shallow promises.

Jack, leaning against the doorframe, smirked.

"Here we go."

And yes, Jack had reappeared too. Sarcasm intact, hair a little thinner, still carrying that air of someone who could solve any problem but would grumble the entire time.

On his first day, he squinted at the tangle of wires under their desks.

"This wiring setup feels like a hacker den from the dial-up era.?"

Sam grinned.

"I am OK with that visual, as long as the Wi-Fi holds."

Their banter slid back into place just like old times.

Then there was Amira Johnson, the new product operations lead.

She was calm, methodical, always carrying her iPad like a shield. She had the aura of someone who had seen processes break before and wasn't about to let it happen again.

At lunch, she turned to Sam.

"We're five people. Four of us are engineers. One PM. Same meetups. Same circles. That's not a culture. That's a mirror."

Sam blinked. He hadn't thought about it that way. He was used to debugging systems, not social dynamics. Amira made him realize both mattered.

First Traces of a Roadmap

The roadmap was fragile, perched between two poles: rewrite versus refactor.

Jack wanted to throw out everything they had in GitHub and rebuild from scratch. Priya argued for prioritizing new features and incremental refactoring. Sam played referee, knowing both were right and both were wrong.

Processes began to appear like seedlings: standups at 9:30, retro every other Friday, an onboarding checklist taped to the wall. Nothing smooth yet, but at least repeatable.

For the first time in years, Sam felt a culture taking shape - not because someone declared it, but because habits formed. Lunch shared. Jokes traded. Bugs cursed in unison.

Without intending to, Sam became the anchor. Juniors drifted toward his desk. He explained patiently, reviewed code late into the night, and redrew the same diagram until they nodded.

He wasn't the founder. But he was becoming the leader.

Valuable Lessons from Metrics

One Friday, a carton of Thai noodles in hand, Sam scribbled on the whiteboard.

"DORA metrics," he wrote.

Jack groaned.

"Another acronym? Shoot me now."

Sam completely sidestepped the sarcasm and continued talking.

"Think sports stats. Not about who's fastest. About how the team plays."

He listed them one by one:

- **Deployment Frequency**: how often we ship.

- **Lead Time**: how long from commit to production.

- **MTTR (Mean Time to Recovery)**: how quickly we recover when things break.

- **CFR (Change Failure Rate)**: how often changes cause issues.

"Batting averages," he said. "One player's speed doesn't matter if the team can't score."

Priya rolled her eyes.

"Sports metaphors. Predictable."

But the following week, Sam overheard her telling the founders: "We're improving our batting average."

Sam sipped his tea and smiled.

The First Stumble into Distributed Work

Their first international contractor joined - a backend engineer from Serbia.

Day one: he joined the stand-up call at 3 a.m. his time, bleary-eyed, mumbling an update before disappearing.

Day two: his mic shrieked feedback so loud that Amira dropped her coffee cup.

Day three: Priya forgot the time zone and scheduled the sprint review for midnight.

Jack muttered, "I thought agile was supposed to make us faster. Instead, we're calendar-wranglers."

Sam shrugged.

"Welcome to distributed work."

They laughed, but Sam knew: this was the future. Better to stumble now than be blindsided later.

Vignettes of Growth

The Build Breaker.
Another junior engineer merged code without review. Staging collapsed. Groans filled the office.

Sam sat beside her, walking her line by line through all the commits. Together they rolled back the changes.

She whispered, "I thought I'd be fired."

"Not for mistakes," Sam said. "Only for not learning from them."

Her relief shone. Sam realized he had shifted from coder to mentor.

The Hackathon.
They entered a local hackathon. This time it wasn't about winning. It was about fun and learning.

They built a real-time fraud engine: when velocity or pattern anomalies spike, it alerts the team and auto-halts the offending source of transactions. Even some "hackers" stopped by after the demo and exclaimed, "whoa."

For the first time, Sam felt the team building *together*, not just him duct-taping alone.

The Lightning Talk#2

At a local meetup, Sam got ambushed. Someone dropped out of the lightning talk lineup, and the organizer shoved a mic into his hand.

"Topic?" Sam asked.

"Anything."

He walked onto the small stage, palms sweaty, and scrawled on the whiteboard: *Lessons from Broken Builds.*

He told the story of a midnight pager, exaggerated the panic of refreshing dashboards, mimed praying to Stack Overflow, and acted out the silence in HipChat when nobody wanted to admit it was their fault.

The crowd laughed. They clapped. They groaned in recognition.

Sam walked off, trembling but smiling. Priya found him at the snack table.

"See? You can pitch - if it's about code, not capital."

Sam chuckled, but her words sank deep. *She's right. This is the stage I want. Teaching, not selling.*

Planting the First Principles

Amira wasn't satisfied with accidental rituals.

"We need values," she said one Wednesday. "Not just rules taped to the wall. Intention."

She handed out sticky notes. "Write one word for how you want this place to feel."

The wall filled quickly:

- Curious.
- Inclusive.
- Fast but forgiving.
- Clarity above all else.

Jack scribbled *DON'T PANIC* in block letters.

Priya wrote *Evidence.*

Sam hesitated, then wrote *Craft.*

Amira read them aloud. "If we keep even half of these, we'll be better than any team in the world, even twice our size."

For the first time, culture felt designed, not accidental.

The Moments That Make a Team

The All-Hands Fire Alarm.
The building alarm blared in the middle of their first company-wide meeting. Everyone stumbled outside. Sam looked around: twenty people on the sidewalk, laughing, swearing, still glued to the updates on their phones.

For the first time, he thought: *We're not a project anymore. We're a company.*

The Night of Ten Bugs.
Sam stayed late with two juniors. Every bug they fixed spawned two more. By 2 a.m., the board looked like a hydra. Sam ordered pizza. They kept going, delirious but determined.

At dawn, staging was stable. One junior muttered, "Best night ever."

Sam believed him.

Product vs. Engineering

Their clashes never stopped. Priya demanded clarity. Sam demanded flexibility.

One day she snapped, "You care more about code elegance than users."

Sam shot back, "And you care more about shiny UX than durability."

The room went silent.

Then she sighed. "Maybe we need both."

Sam chuckled. "Don't tell Jack. He'll gloat."

Their arguments softened after that - still fiery, but productive. They had become sparring partners instead of adversaries.

Still Distributed, But Beginning to Align

The Eastern European contractor settled in, but remote life stayed messy: Chat message alerts at 3 a.m., time zone misses, bug reports in half-translated English.

Jack groaned. "Agile was supposed to make us faster. Instead, I'm living in Google Calendar."

Sam grinned. "Congratulations. You've leveled up to the Calendar Cowboy title."

Even the contractor laughed.

Constellations in the Dark

Late one Thursday night, Sam lingered. The office was quiet, screens glowing like constellations in the dark.

The sprint board still looked messy. Bugs remained. Deadlines pressed. But the air carried something different - laughter that lingered after mistakes, respect after arguments, trust after late nights.

He opened his notebook and wrote in his cramped scrawl: *I finally hit a stride that feels sustainable.*

For the first time in years, Sam was comfortable operating in his own lane. Not pitching. Not pretending. Just building.

Closing Business Snapshot

Stage	Formation Stage
Company Value	$5 M (Post-Seed)
ARR	$500k
Annual Profit	- $300k
Total Funding Raised	$1million
Total Employees	~20
Eng Employees	8
Sam's Equity	4% (Unvested)
Infra Bill	$15k/month

Concept Learned: DORA Metrics

DORA metrics reframed what engineering excellence meant for Sam. Traditional management obsessed over visible effort - sprint velocity, burn-down rates, utilization percentages. All those signals measured motion, not progress.

The DORA framework flipped the lens. It asked one simple question: *how fast can we safely learn from change?*

- **Deployment Frequency:** Are we confident enough to ship daily or even more often?

- **Lead Time for Changes:** Are ideas trapped in review queues or flowing to users?

- **MTTR:** When things break, do we recover in minutes or days?

- **Change Failure Rate:** Are our experiments reliable or reckless?

These metrics didn't reward perfection; instead, they celebrated adaptability.

How Sam Amplified Engineering Metrics

Sam introduced DORA metrics in conversation, not simply through official dashboards.
He compared deployments to practice drills - frequent reps build strength, long pauses cause stiffness.
At first the team rolled their eyes, but soon they started asking, "What slowed this push?" instead of, "Who caused the delay?"

Data replaced blame. Recovery became teamwork.
The group's rhythm shifted from defensive to curious - less about avoiding mistakes, more about shortening the time between them.

By the end of that quarter, Sam noticed a subtle cultural change: engineers started finishing sentences with *"Let's measure it."* That, more than any chart, told him the idea had landed.

Chapter 5

The First Real Team

The announcement hit like a summer thunderclap. One minute, the office hummed with the Monday rhythm of keyboards and espresso shots; the next, a Slack ping detonated across every screen: *Series A CLOSED*.

Someone screamed from the back corner, "We did it!" Another person popped a bottle that had been chilling in the office fridge since Christmas. Champagne and sparkling cider frothed onto keyboards. Glitter cannons coughed confetti into ceiling fans. For a few chaotic seconds, the room sounded like victory itself.

Sam cheered, too - because everyone did - but deep inside, he felt that quiet tug of caution that comes only from experience. He had seen early triumphs turn brittle before. Funding meant headcount, and headcount meant management. Growth didn't just amplify success; it also amplified complexity & confusion.

An hour later, his calendar pinged:

3:00 PM - Transition Plan for Sam → Engineering Manager.

He frowned. A promotion meeting he hadn't requested.

Series A and the Promotion He Didn't Ask For

Jonas Lee, the company's CTO, was waiting in the corner conference room. He was the calmest person Sam had ever met - silver at the temples, sneakers that somehow still looked formal, voice like a metronome that refused to speed up.

"Sam," Jonas said, sliding a folder across the table, "you've been leading without a title. Time you got one. Well-deserved"

Sam opened the folder. Inside sat an org chart, a promotion offer letter, and a job description dense with verbs: *coach, prioritize, deliver, mentor.*

He exhaled. "I just wanted to code."

Jonas smiled. "You still will. Some. But now your code compiles through people."

Sam stared at the signature line, feeling the weight of it. "So this is official?"

"As official as it gets," Jonas replied.

He signed, the pen leaving a faint smear of ink where his hand trembled.

The next morning, he arrived early - coffee in one hand, anxiety in the other. The office smelled like paint and warm bagels. Twenty people now filled what had once been ten. He noticed something subtle: half the new faces looked at him before deciding where to sit. Authority was invisible until suddenly it wasn't.

Priya caught his eye over her monitor. "Morning, Boss."

He winced. "Don't."

She grinned. "Then act like you're not."

That became their rhythm: teasing honesty disguised as banter.

Later that week, Ava Patel joined as the new senior product designer - creative, brisk, composed. On her first day she said, "I can forgive ugly code. But I will never forgive ugly user flows."

Sam grinned. "Then I'll make sure our bugs are beautifully aligned."

Ava raised an eyebrow. "Alignment is not beauty. Beauty is intention."

"Then we'll align our intentions beautifully," he corrected.

She laughed, conceding the point. "Good save. We might get along."

They clicked immediately - two perfectionists speaking in different dialects of the same obsession. For the next hour they hovered over a whiteboard, debating button placements like diplomats negotiating a fragile treaty. At one point Sam said, "If we keep refining this flow, we're going to redesign the entire product today."

Ava conceded. "Fine by me. That's what ecosystems do - they evolve."

The team was getting larger, louder, but it felt like an ecosystem.

Learning Under the Weight of Management

By spring, the company had doubled. New monitors and Herman-Miller chairs arrived weekly; employee handbooks and welcome packets stacked like menus at a diner. The whiteboards groaned under sprint plans and architecture doodles that nobody erased. Sam loved the noise - the sound of creation - but beneath it pulsed an undercurrent of panic. For every new feature, another broke. For every hire, another process wobbled.

He began keeping a notebook titled *Manager Bugs*.

The first few entries were jokes:

- How to give feedback without sounding like a parent.
- How to end meetings before morale expires.
- How to estimate when everything is "80% done" perpetually

By Friday, the list had more pages than his actual bug tracker.

Jonas called an all-hands meeting to "align on post-Series A priorities." Sam stood beside him at the front, pulse quickening as he realized everyone was waiting for him to speak.

"We're entering a new phase," he began. "More users, more features, more... everything." Nervous chuckles rippled through the crowd. "But remember - funding doesn't change physics. We still ship one deploy at a time."

A small laugh spread, and he exhaled. When the meeting ended, Ava clapped his shoulder. "Not bad for your first sermon."

"Was it that obvious I was winging it?"

"Completely," she said.

Later that week, Sam held his first official one-on-one with a junior engineer. He asked questions, got monosyllables, and ended the chat within seven awkward minutes. Two more one-on-ones later, that engineer quit without warning. Sam replayed the conversations as if they were failed unit tests, eventually realizing he'd treated them like necessary transactions instead of two humans connecting.

He started scheduling longer check-ins, bringing snacks, and learning to let silence work. It helped - barely.

At night, he missed the clarity of interacting with code. Variables didn't misunderstand intent. Functions didn't burn out. He bought a peace lily for his desk, a reminder to breathe. Jack promptly renamed it *Deadlock*.

"Perfect mascot," Jack said. "Looks alive until you forget to water it."

Sam smirked. "You just summarized half our system."

He added a new note in *Manager Bugs*: *Plants and people both need consistent watering.*

Hiring and Firing as Design Problems

The funding-inspired hiring season hit like a storm. Two weeks after his promotion, Sam found himself in back-to-back interviews. He still remembered the chaos of early hiring - the coffee-shop promises, the gut calls that aged badly into regrets. This time, he wanted rigor.

He built a spreadsheet labeled *Candidate Rubric v1.0*, with weighted columns: Communication (20%), Debugging (30%), System Design (30%), Collaboration (20%). Everyone interviewing filled it out. No exceptions.

Jack peeked over his shoulder. "You turned hiring into algebra. Where's the fun in that?"

"Math's less biased than memory," Sam said.

The rigor worked. They started hiring better fits faster, avoiding charm-based mistakes. Jonas stopped by his desk after one panel. "You just saved us six months of regret," he said quietly.

Then came the test of leadership no rubric could prepare him for.

Nikhil, a mid-level engineer, hadn't opened a Pull Request in 5 weeks and stopped engaging in other engineers' reviews. The team whispered; release cadence veered off. Sam scheduled a meeting and practiced the script in his notebook: *Be kind. Be clear. Be brief.*

"I can see you trying," Sam began carefully, "but the pace isn't matching the role. We've paired, swapped projects, and coached. It's still not landing."

Nikhil looked down. "You're firing me."

Sam paused. "I'm ending a mismatch. You deserve a place that fits better."

A long silence followed, broken only by the hum of the AC. Then a small nod. "Thank you for saying it straight."

After he left, Sam sat in the empty room until Jack found him. "First one?" Jack asked.

Sam nodded.

"If it ever stops hurting," Jack said, "that's when you worry."

The next morning, the office felt lighter - sad but aligned.

He wrote in his notebook: *Firing fast isn't cruelty. It's clarity.*

Months later, when another underperformer struggled, Sam handled it differently.

He coached the engineer in real-time, documented the journey diligently, supported them through slip-ups and triumphs - and when the end was imminent, he had a recommendation letter ready along with a 3-month severance package. The engineer replied with a note Sam would never delete: *Thanks for treating me like a fellow human, not a low priority Jira ticket.*

That single sentence taught him more about leadership than any book on leadership.

Building Team Identity and Culture

Jonas declared a weeklong off-site, *"Team bonding,"* he said.

They rented a creaky lodge near Mt. Hood, the kind that smelled like wood smoke and stale cocoa. Snow clung to the trees outside, and someone packed three times more snacks & La Croix than necessary.

The first day started with icebreakers.

Jack introduced himself as "resident cynic, recovering perfectionist." Priya followed: "Product manager. Professional translator of unrealistic expectations." When it was Sam's turn, he said, "I'm the guy who fixes your merge conflicts and your moods."
Laughter rippled. The tension broke.

For their last night, they gathered around a campfire while flakes of snow fell like ash. Jonas passed around mugs of cocoa and asked each person to share one thing they'd learned.

Priya said, "Leadership is explaining the same thing twelve times without sounding tired." Jack proclaimed, "Velocity's a feeling, not a number."

Ava emphasized, "Design is empathy made visible."

When it was Sam's turn, he stared into the flames. "I used to think code was logic and people were chaos," he said. "Turns out people have patterns too - you just have to read a very different set of logs."

They went quiet. Then someone murmured, "Ship it."

Back in Portland, Sam started Friday fifteen-minute check-ins. No laptops, just conversation. He asked one question: *"What's slowing you down?"* Sometimes it was code; more often, confidence. He learned that mentoring wasn't teaching - it was listening until someone heard themselves think.

A junior engineer once admitted, "I'm afraid to implement Priya's workflow designs. They are too... elegant."

Sam chuckled. "Good code isn't porcelain. It's playground equipment. Use it till it squeaks."

A week later, that same engineer submitted a pull request to Priya's favorite workflow. Priya commented, *Thanks for improving the playground.* Sam printed it and taped it in his notebook.

The peace lily, *Deadlock,* somehow remained alive. Ava began sticking Post-its to the pot - *remember 1:1 with Nikhil 2.0, buy real coffee filters.*

It became a running joke that the plant was the real project manager. When new hires joined, someone would point and say, "Better ask Deadlock if you're stuck."

Culture had arrived - not through HR decks, but through inside jokes.

One evening, Priya stopped by Sam's desk. "You still look like you're choosing between oxygen and gravity."

He blinked. "Meaning?"

"You keep trying to pick between being an engineer and a manager. You don't have to choose. You lead every time you teach, argue, or write clear code. Titles are lagging indicators."

That line stuck in his head like a perfectly optimized ruby function. He wrote it down before leaving that evening. *Titles are lagging indicators.* He didn't know it yet, but it would follow him for years.

Scaling, Structure, and Sustainable Pace

Autumn arrived with new MacBooks, more new names in Slack, and a calendar that looked like an error log. Engineering had tripled.

Departments sprouted: Quality, DevOps, ProductOps, Program Management, Security - each with their own rituals and meeting cadences.

Jonas paced during Monday leadership sync. "We need to 10x our velocity," he said. "More customers, more features, faster shipping."

Sam rubbed his temples. "Velocity isn't a metric we amplify at will - it's the flow behind the features."

Jonas leaned forward, curious and agitated at the same time. "Unpack that for me"

"Add people too quickly and you get speed without traction," Sam said. "Tires spinning in mud."

Ava nodded. "And mud ruins the paint."

Laughter lightened the room, but the truth sat between them: growth was no longer elegant. Every new hire dramatically increased the number of conversations required to make even a simple decision.

Later that day, Sam gathered his senior engineers. "You've heard of The Mythical Man-Month, right?" Blank stares. He drew a kitchen on the whiteboard - one turkey, one oven, twenty chefs.

"You can't cook dinner faster by hiring more chefs," he said. "You just run out of counter space."

Jack raised a hand. "So fewer chefs, more ovens?"

"Exactly. Parallelize the work, not the people."

Priya leaned in the doorway. "Can we put that in the onboarding doc under *Sam's Laws of Physics Defied*?"

"Only if it comes with a Venn diagram," Jack said.

Within a week, the meme spread across Slack like shorthand. Anytime projects overloaded, someone typed: *Too many chefs....* and everyone understood.

Jonas approved a restructure - smaller, autonomous pods, four developers max. The first two sprints were chaotic. Ownership blurred, releases collided, API contracts broke. But in a month, something clicked. PR reviews got faster. Incidents dropped. Engineers started smiling again.

Priya called it "the calm after the merge."

Ava painted a mural on the wall: *Build small. Ship often. Learn out loud.*

Sam stood before it one morning, coffee in hand, realizing he finally bought into it.

He launched *Tuesday Swaps* - pairing seniors and juniors for an hour of shadowing. Jack christened it "babysitting." A month later, he grudgingly admitted he'd learned more by sharing than coding. Sam watched the feedback loops take shape: questions turning into patterns, patterns into culture.

When burnout flared, Sam tried a new rule: *Quiet Week*. No meetings, only asynchronous updates. Panic at first, then productivity. Jonas frowned at the metrics. "Why are stand-ups down forty percent?"

"Because people are standing less and producing more," Sam said.

Jonas laughed. "Fine. You win this round too."

One day, Ava wandered to his desk, where he was updating a messy architecture diagram. "Trying to predict the future again?"

"Every arrow I draw creates three more meetings," he sighed.

"That's how you know you're leading," she said. "The lines matter now."

He smiled faintly. "Sometimes I miss the simplicity of code."

"Then teach them simplicity," she said. "That's still code - just collaboratively written for people."

He thought about that for a long time after she left.

The First Real Team, Celebrated

Three months later, the founders hosted an official Series A celebration at a rooftop bar downtown. String lights hung between patio heaters. A jazz trio played slightly off tempo. People wore their "startup formal" best: engineers in ironed shirts, Priya in a sharp blazer, Jack in a T-shirt that read *I Fix Things That Aren't Broken Yet*.

Jonas clinked his glass. "To the next phase - our unicorn status and beyond!"

The crowd roared.

Sam smiled, lifted his drink, and stayed near the edge. Portland shimmered below them like a circuit board, each window a tiny diode of light.

Ava joined him, holding a glass of sparkling water. "You look proud," she said.

"I am," he admitted. "Also terrified."

"Good combination," she said. "Keeps the bugs down."

Jack wandered over, already flushed. "Manager or not, you're still the guy we call when prod is on fire."

Priya raised her glass. "To Sam - the reluctant Manager who learned empathy is a feature."

Laughter and cheers erupted.

Sam laughed, too - a real laugh, born of exhaustion and gratitude. For the first time in months, he wasn't just managing; he was belonging.

As the night thinned and the band packed up, Sam stepped toward the balcony. The air smelled faintly of rain and ozone. The city pulsed quietly below. He whispered, "I hope we're ready. Because now the game really begins."

He didn't mean it as a warning. He meant it as faith.

Closing Business Snapshot

Stage	Series A - Year 3
Company Value	$50 M (post Series A)
ARR	$2 M run-rate
Annual Profit	– $1.2 M
Funding Raised	$11 million
Total Employees	40
Engineering Employees	12
Sam's Equity	3.8% (50% vested)
Infra Bill	$25k/month

Concept Learned: Team Topologies

Sam learned what every scaling company eventually does: adding people doesn't linearly add output - it multiplies communication paths. The constraint on velocity isn't hardware or process; it's human interaction bandwidth.

Fred Brooks called it out decades ago in *The Mythical Man-Month*: nine women can't deliver a baby in one month. Sam rediscovered that principle the hard way. Each new hire added overhead - coordination meetings, code reviews, onboarding loops - until "help" became drag.

He found a modern lens in the Team Topologies framework: design teams around the flow of work, not the org chart. Stream-aligned squads own distinct user value; enabling teams provide shared tools; platform teams standardize common services. The model treats communication as architecture - something to be shaped, not endured.

How Sam Orchestrated Team Topologies

He redrew the org map into a set of small, autonomous squads. Each had a clear mission, one cross-functional owner, and minimal dependencies. Instead of managing coordination, they managed boundaries.

"You can't debug faster by adding more engineers to the same terminal - you just end up with terrible merge conflicts in real life."

The line stuck. Another meme spread across Slack, then as shorthand for focus.

Within months, handoffs dropped, morale rose, and releases doubled without chaos. Jonas called it *operational elegance*. Sam just called it breathing room - the moment when growth finally felt sustainable.

Chapter 6

Craft in the Crosshairs of Context

The company, AtlasPay Systems no longer smelled of dust, takeout, and secondhand ambitions. It smelled like polish. Varnished floors. Fresh coffee ground in small ceremonial batches. The ozone-tinted hum of new hardware. By then they occupied two full floors of the converted warehouse - glass conference rooms, clean lines, branded signage, and a cheerful digital assistant at reception that greeted visitors by name. Sam remembered the days when they joked about ever needing a receptionist. Now they had one - and it was voice-activated.

He stood in the elevator lobby one morning, watching forty-odd employees filter through badge readers. Designers with noise-canceling headphones. Product managers clutching their craft kombucha. Engineers nerding out about their road bicycles. It was the kind of growth curve founders celebrated on stage, but he felt something else under the surface: a faint vibration of unease, like the hum that precedes feedback in an audio system.

He used to measure progress in commits and database size. In the early days, he could take a side glance at a pull request and instantly grade the reliability, security and quality of the outcome. He knew where tension lived in the codebase the same way a musician senses which string is a hair off pitch.

Now progress arrived in a different form: performance reviews, quarterly planning spreadsheets, org charts, conversations about leveling frameworks, documentation audits, and all-hands decks. His desk - once cluttered with mechanical keyboards and Raspberry Pi experiments - was now crowded with notebooks filled with half-written feedback notes and to-do lists that reproduced themselves like invasive weeds.

Every promotion, Sam realized, traded clarity for altitude.

And up there, the air felt thinner.

Still, the pride was real. The company had traction. Investors called weekly. A rumor floated through the hallway that a Series B might be "closer than leadership was letting on." People were excited. People believed in the vision.

But belief, Sam knew, wasn't enough to hold a system together.

At his desk, he slid into his chair and watched the morning stand-up unfold. Priya moderated with her usual blend of firmness and grace. Jack brought his signature sarcasm but with the reliability Sam had come to depend on. Lena's team walked through the status of the API redesign. A new intern timidly shared an update and received a chorus of supportive nods.

It should have felt triumphant.

Instead, Sam felt like an exile from his own craft - near enough to hear the familiar music, too far to play an instrument.

The Pull of the Keyboard

The tug toward code started as an itch.

A quiet whisper: *Just review one pull request. Just check the sentry error logs. Just a peek.*

After dinner, the room dim and still, Sam would open his laptop with what he told himself were harmless intentions. The screen's blue glow filled the room like an old addiction returning. One review became two. Two became three. A small suggestion drifted into a tiny refactor. He rationalized every change: *It's mentorship. It's harmless. It's faster this way.*

But the truth pressed in quietly: he was afraid of drifting too far from the craft.

By two in the morning, he would close the laptop with the faint shame of someone caught reliving a habit they'd sworn off. He crawled into bed and told himself he'd do better tomorrow.

Of course, he didn't.

Priya noticed and confronted him first.

She appeared at his desk one morning with two lattes - one sweetened, one bitter - and handed him the bitter one like a prescription.

"When you say 'delegation,'" she asked, "does that include rewriting people's code at 2:00 am?"

Sam blinked. "I was just reviewing."

"Reviewing is feedback," she said. "What you're doing is repossession."

Her voice wasn't sharp. It was disappointing. Tired. The tone of a friend who'd watched him try to split himself between two incompatible identities.

"You can't be half a manager forever," she said. "Lead or code. Pick one."

She left him with the bitter latte and a silence so heavy it felt like a heavy plate on his chest.

That night, he kept the laptop closed.

The silence felt worse than debugging a production crash.

Stand-ups ran smoothly.

Retros ended tidily.

Jira boards moved in a rhythm he could almost predict.

But predictability, he discovered, came with a tax.

He missed the improvisational chaos - the thrill of discovery that lived behind every commit in the early days.

He wasn't nostalgic for the struggle. He was nostalgic for the clarity.

One day, during a planning meeting, he looked down at his notebook and realized with a jolt that he had written nothing but meeting agendas for an entire week. No sketches of ideal architecture ideas. No glimpses of future systems. No code. Just logistics.

The realization sat in his stomach like a rock.

He wanted to lead.

He just didn't know how to stop being the engineer whose identity had always been built on output.

Sam looked around the room - Lena presenting a migration plan, Jack making a dry joke about error budgets, Priya explaining user flows - and thought, *they're not waiting for your commits anymore. They're waiting for your clarity.*

And for the first time, he wasn't sure he knew how to give it.

Controlled Combustion

Quarterly planning had begun to resemble an organized argument rather than a meeting.

Product wanted acceleration: ambitious features, aggressive timelines, a future painted in bold strokes.

Engineering wanted breathing room: upgrades to legacy modules, refactors long overdue, load testing that everyone knew mattered, all of that without a set schedule.

The CEO wanted both. Immediately.

The conference room felt tight, even with its twelve-foot ceilings. Sunlight pooled on the concrete floors like molten gold, bouncing against glass and amplifying the friction in the air.

"We need the revamped merchant onboarding flow live before the end of the quarter," the CEO insisted, tapping the whiteboard as if that added emphasis.

Jack, half-hidden behind his laptop, muttered just loud enough to register, "Sure. If the codebase doesn't collapse in protest."

Priya tried diplomacy, walking the room through dependencies with her steady voice. But she ended up stuck in a crossfire of executive urgency and engineering reality.

Sam listened, feeling the pressure build. Every voice tugged at a different corner of the roadmap: growth, performance, stability, user delight, customer demands, investor expectations. Every request implied invisible work someone else would have to absorb.

Finally, he raised his hand, steady and quiet.

"Fire needs oxygen," he said. "Too much fire, we burn out. Too much oxygen, nothing lights. The trick is controlled combustion."

The room went silent, the kind of silence where people actually think instead of waiting to argue.

Priya broke it with a crooked smile. "Controlled combustion. I like it."

Someone wrote the phrase on the whiteboard.

Then circled it.

Then underlined it.

It stayed there all quarter - their unofficial philosophy, a reminder that intensity without space collapses systems, and space without intensity stalls them.

But harmony never lasts long in fast-growing companies. Two weeks later, the pressure cracked.

During a retrospective, Jack shut his laptop with a sharp snap. "This isn't engineering anymore," he said. "It's toxic performative theater."

Sam tried to keep calm. "Feedback is part of the process."

"Process?" Jack's laugh was thin. "You've become a gatekeeper. Every decision needs your blessing. You hired thinkers, Sam. Not typists."

He stood, grabbed his bag, and walked out, the door latch echoing more loudly than any shouted argument.

Sam sat there, expression still, pulse loud.

Inside, something caved in.

That evening, at home, he opened a fresh page in his notebook and wrote one line until the ink began to blur:

Let go or lose them.

Delegation by Fire

The next morning, Sam forced himself to do something profoundly uncomfortable: he delegated something fragile!

A mission-critical database migration, one he would have clutched tightly months earlier, went to Lena, newly promoted and still learning to carry her authority.

"You're in charge," he said.

Her eyebrows lifted. "Seriously? You'll let me run point?"

"I'll try," he said, half-smiling.

Over the next six days, Lena led flawlessly. She rehearsed the rollout, triple-checked queries, and coordinated every dependency with quiet confidence.

On day seven, something slipped.

A misconfigured script took the login API offline.

Dashboards erupted red.

Slack detonated.

PagerDuty screamed.

Jonas messaged one word: Status?

Sam typed the only answer that mattered: Lena's leading recovery.

Then he removed his hands from the keyboard. Literally removed them - folded them together, fingers interlocked, a physical barrier to his instinct to intervene.

Every muscle in his body tingled with the pressure of restraint.

Lena triaged.

Lena patched.

Lena coordinated.

Lena restored the system.

Lena led.

Twenty-six minutes later, green bars returned to the dashboard.

Thirty minutes later, the system stabilized.

Thirty-two minutes later, Sam finally exhaled.

He'd survived something harder than any production outage: not being the savoir of the day.

At the post-mortem, Lena owned every line of the breakdown, every contributing factor, every recovery step. Her final slide read:

Trust given is trust tested.

Sam walked to the board and wrote underneath it:

Trust magnified.

Then he bought donuts for the team - not just as a celebration, but as a symbolic gesture of his own growth (obviously he didn't share that!)

Jack, who had returned with a sheepish half-grin that morning, pointed at the pink box. "Ah yes. Carbs, the true apology language."

The room laughed. Tension dissipated.

Every company has moments of fracture.

This one had become a moment of formation.

Later that afternoon, Jonas found Sam in the break room, staring at the mugs as if they contained philosophical answers.

"Heard you didn't jump in," Jonas said.

"Hardest thirty minutes of my life."

"That's leadership," Jonas replied. "Sweating quietly while others learn loudly."

He stirred his espresso, watching Sam over the rim of the cup. "Remember this: leadership isn't a promotion. It's a profession."

The words landed deeper than Sam expected.

Architecture of Trust

To prove - to himself and the team - that he meant what he said, Sam created the Architecture Council. Four leads. One product partner. One designer when needed. No hierarchy. No final approver. Just a forum where people who understood the system could debate, reason, argue, and arrive at aligned decisions.

Jack dubbed it "Nerd Parliament."

Priya preferred "House of Merge."

Ava attended the first session with a sketchbook and a raised eyebrow.

The Council worked.

Not instantly.

Not perfectly.

But steadily.

Engineers brought rough ideas.

Architectural debates sharpened into shared clarity.

Design-informed technical feasibility.

Product understood tradeoffs earlier instead of during crisis.

Soon, the company adopted new language:

"What did the Council decide?"

"Let's bring it to the Council."

"Council review before building."

The bottleneck dissolved.

The role of "final decider" dissolved with it.

For the first time, Sam felt himself becoming replaceable.

At first, that sensation frightened him.

Then it comforted him.

Leadership wasn't about being the center.

It was about making that center redundant.

Every week, the system needed Sam 5% less.

And for the first time in his professional life, needing him less meant the org was succeeding more.

Layering the Leader

On Thursday mornings, Sam and Ava met at the little café across the street - two blocks from the office, a world away from the polished ambition inside it. The café was imperfect in all the ways Sam secretly preferred: uneven tables, chipped ceramic mugs, a too-loud grinder that overwhelmed conversations, and a messy chalkboard menu that never matched the ingredients in stock.

It was their ritual. Caffeine and clarity.

One gray morning, with rain misting the windows and soft jazz humming in the background, Sam admitted what he hadn't said aloud to anyone.

"Letting go feels like erasing myself," he said, fingers tracing the rim of his mug. "I used to gauge my worth by what I built. By the lines of code I wrote. Now everything I do is... invisible. Meetings. Decisions. Nudges. Listening."

Ava didn't look up from her sketchbook. She was drawing, as always - loops, boxes, flows - turning thought into shapes.

"You're not erasing anything," she said. "You're layering. Designers do it all the time. You draw the first version, then trace over the parts that matter. You refine. You hide the scaffolding. That's how the final thing becomes clear."

"So, I'm a refactor of myself?" he asked, an embarrassed smile bent at the edges.

She glanced at him sharply. "Exactly. You're committing Sam 2.0."

The metaphor struck deeper than any leadership workshop ever had. He felt something shift - not a revelation, but a re-alignment. A sense that the foundation he thought he was losing was actually evolving into something broader, stronger, more structural.

Later that evening, back at the office long after the day's bustle died, Sam sat alone with a single lamp illuminating his desk. The hum of server fans filled the quiet, their steady drone grounding him.

On the screen was an empty Confluence page titled:

Engineering Career Ladder - Draft 0.1

He began typing slowly, carefully:

- Learner - builds with guidance; asks good questions.
- Builder - delivers independently; documents as they go.
- Craftsman - improves systems they didn't write.
- Mentor - multiplies others' impact.
- Architect - designs context, not code.

And then, after a long pause, the final line:

- Leader - tunes the orchestra so others can play.

He sat back. The ladder was both a blueprint for his team and a confession for himself. A map of the journey he'd taken, and the one he was still climbing.

To be honest it was not quite a neatly designed ladder as much as a jungle gym. And that was more than OK.

He tagged Jonas and Ava for comments.

Saved the document.

Then closed the laptop - and for the first time in months, didn't take it home.

The hallway lights dimmed to night mode.

The office breathed in its sleep.

And Sam walked out lighter than he'd arrived.

The Orchestra Moment of Truth

Winter settled into the city with quiet insistence - cold rain, wind sharpening at corners, streetlights flickering against puddles. Inside the warehouse headquarters, the company was different now. Not calmer. Not slower. But more self-assured - with feedback loops instead of bottlenecks, shared context instead of central dependency.

Sam walked the aisles, coffee in hand, soaking it in.

- Lena coached a junior through writing cleaner tests.
- Jack explained a new logging framework with surprising patience.
- Priya rehearsed a roadmap pitch, words flowing with controlled precision.
- Ava reviewed a design prototype, pencil tapping as she cut unnecessary complexity.

Nobody was waiting on Sam.

Nobody hovered.

Nobody sought permission.

The company had developed its own pulse.

A friend from San Francisco visited one afternoon. After a brief tour, he asked casually, "What's changed the most since the early days?"

Sam looked around, watching his team move with coordination that hadn't existed a year earlier.

"I used to write code," he said. "Now we nurture builders who create products."

It sounded dramatic even to his own ears, but it was true.
Systems scale when people mature. Teams thrive when trust becomes structural.

A week later, at the weekly all-hands, Sam walked onto the small stage at the front of the open space. Someone had mischievously added a tiny conductor emoji next to his name on the agenda slide. He rolled his eyes with a smile but didn't remove it.

Everyone quieted.

"Engineering Managers," he began, "aren't bosses."

A few eyebrows raised. Jack leaned forward from the back row.

"Think of an EM as a conductor," Sam continued. "You don't play the violin anymore. You don't hammer the drums. You listen. You pace. You tune the room. You make sure the violins don't drown the trumpets. The goal isn't to be the loudest. It's to help the team play in harmony."

A ripple of laughter moved through the crowd.

Jack screamed, "Do we get tuxedos?"

Sam grinned. "After Series B."

Even Jonas cracked a rare smile.

Something internal settled into place then - not a victory, not relief, but recognition. He wasn't giving up being an engineer. He was expanding the definition.

He wasn't writing code anymore - he was refining context.

He wasn't refactoring logic - he was renewing relationships.

He wasn't debugging systems - he was upleveling teams.

And the music that resulted was fuller, richer, and far more resilient than anything he could have produced alone.

A Company That Breathes on Its Own

That evening, long after most of the team had left, Sam lingered by the bullpen area. Monitors glowed like distant campfires. A couple of engineers debated test coverage thresholds in low voices. A design mockup glowed on a projector left running. Someone's half-eaten granola bar sat next to a whiteboard diagram about caching layers.

It was peaceful. Not quiet - but peaceful.

Priya passed him on her way to the elevator, her bag slung over her shoulder.

"You didn't open VSCode today?" she said.

He smiled. "Didn't need to."

She nodded, approving. "That's the job."

Sam looked back at the rows of desks, the gentle glow of monitors, the hum of a team that had learned to self-regulate. And he understood, finally, what scale truly meant.

The company could breathe - without him counting.

He stepped into the elevator, let the doors close, and felt a strange mix of pride and grief. He had built something he no longer needed to hold. And that was the point.

Closing Business Snapshot

Stage	Late Series A → Early Series B
Company Value	$78 M (Valuation)
ARR	$5 M
Annual Profit	– $2.4 M
Total Funding Raised	$11million
Total Employees	50
Eng Employees	20
Sam's Equity	3.4% (Fully vested)
Infra Bill	$40k/month

Concept Learned: Delegation & Career Ladders

Sam realized, almost reluctantly, that his leadership struggles had the same root cause as many technical failures he had debugged over the years: over coupling. He had become an invisible monolith - every decision passing through him, every dependency anchored to him. The team scaled, but he did not. Because of that, the system strained.

Delegation, he discovered, wasn't simply "letting go."
It was *architecting flow*.

Good software systems scale when their components have clean boundaries, stable interfaces, and minimal friction. Good teams scale for the same reason.

He began reframing leadership as a design problem:

- People are not "reports" - they're *services* with clear domains.
- Meetings weren't ceremonies - they were *sync jobs*.
- Conflicts weren't personal - they were *interface mismatches*.
- Documentation wasn't bureaucracy - it was a shared *context that prevents drift*.

And that's where the Career Ladder clicked into place. It became the equivalent of an API contract for human growth: predictable, explicit, evolution friendly.

Just as a well-written API spec tells you *how to integrate with a system*, a well-written ladder tells engineers *how to integrate with a company's growth*.

The moment this analogy landed, Sam understood leadership in a new way: scaling the product required scaling himself first.

How Sam Precisely Scaled Career Ladders

He started modeling his team like a distributed architecture:

- Each engineer owned a domain, with autonomy guarded as intentionally as microservice boundaries.
- Retros and one-on-ones operated like recurring heartbeat signals - steady, periodic, low friction.
- The newly formed Architecture Council functioned as the orchestrator, routing context to the place where expertise lived instead of where authority sat.
- And the Career Ladder became the documentation layer of this system - the glossary, the schema, the shared mental model.

Engineers adopted the vocabulary almost immediately:
"I think I'm moving from Builder to Craftsperson."
"Mentorship was my missing rep."
"This project earned me my first Architect-level decision."

It spread faster than any memo Sam had ever written.
Within weeks, meetings were shortened.
Ownership sharpened.
Decision-making decentralized.
Sam's inbox lightened.

And one Friday afternoon, staring at the sprint board, he realized something startling: he had not been the bottleneck all week. For the first time, leadership felt like clean code: readable, reliable, and running in production with just a handful of exceptions.

Chapter 7

Scaling Pains

The Advent of Hypergrowth

The morning after the Series B announcement, the office felt like someone had tried to freeze joy into architecture. Balloons clung to the ceiling like multicolored barnacles. A vinyl banner stretched across the stairwell - HYPERGROWTH STARTS HERE - printed in a font that could only have been designed by someone who had never lived through hypergrowth. A stack of sparkling wine bottles sat beside the coffee machine, which hissed aggressively as if irritated by the celebration.

Jonas stepped out onto the mezzanine, rang a small brass bell, and shouted, "30-million raised!"

Applause exploded upward. HR filmed everything. Recruiters hovered near the back, already lining up interviews. For a moment, Sam felt the surge too - pride, relief, the sense that the years of grinding and uncertainty were finally validated.

But then the applause ended, and the real noise began.

Laptops arrived in bulk shipments. Desks crowded into corners. The People Ops team sprinted through hallways with onboarding folders like medics at a battlefield triage. Slack channels multiplied so quickly Sam had to mute half of them. Engineering stand-ups doubled in size. New hires joined daily - many before Sam could even learn their names. The company that once felt like a tight-knit crew now felt like a city being built faster than its streets could be mapped.

Growth wasn't a steady stream anymore; it was an avalanche.

Dashboards Here... There... Everywhere

The first dashboard appeared the week after Series B - an innocuous rotation of DORA metrics: deployment frequency, mean time to recovery, change failure rate. Sam nodded approvingly. They needed visibility.

The second dashboard arrived two days later. Then a third. Soon the walls were studded with screens: uptime graphs glowing like ECG monitors, conversion funnels pulsing like neon lungs, and sprint velocity charts blinking with the intensity of casino slot machines.

Every stand-up began with numbers. Every retro circled back to numbers. Every product review meeting ended with a debate about numbers. If a chart wasn't green, the room tensed.

Two engineers whispered near Sam's desk one morning.
"If we just raise the story-point estimate on that epic, our velocity looks way healthier," one said.

Sam stopped mid-step. "That's not estimation - that's inflation."
They froze, embarrassed. But he knew they weren't alone.

Metrics had stopped being diagnostic and started being decorative. The dashboards were makeup - concealing fatigue with color.

Even Priya, who once argued passionately for user clarity, now spoke in numbers. "If we hit fifty deployments this month, that metric will pop out in our board deck," she said one afternoon, tapping her laptop like a talisman.

"Deploying garbage still counts as a deployment?" Sam said.

She sighed dramatically. "Don't ruin the vibe."

He let it slide, but the unease settled deeper.

Breaking Under the Pace

By midsummer, headcount soared past 150. It felt impressive until Sam noticed the subtler signals: laughter thinning, shoulders slumping, conversations shortening.

Layoffs followed suit not too far behind.

Jonas called Sam into his office one gray Monday. Sunlight slanted across the room in an accusatory way, spotlighting the single sheet of paper on the table. "We have to reduce burn," Jonas said quietly. "Fifteen percent across departments."

Sam blinked. "Fifteen?"

"I wish it were less."

The ache that followed wasn't sharp; it was slow, diffused - a bruise forming beneath the skin.

That Friday, Sam stood in front of the engineering team as faces blurred behind screens and tears. "This isn't about performance," he said. "This is about keeping our dream alive." He hated how rehearsed it sounded, even though he had rewritten the speech twelve times.

The layoffs lasted a whole day. The grief lasted much longer.

That evening Sam sat alone at his desk, staring at the chairs left empty. A few potted plants and hand-written sticky notes remained like artifacts from a civilization that had vanished overnight. He knew companies were supposed to rebound - replace seats, refill Slack channels, move on. But something fundamental had shifted. Trust had cracked.

The remaining engineers worked harder, not because they believed more but because fear worked faster than inspiration. Slack statuses quietly changed from "online" to "invisible." Cameras during stand-up were "off for bandwidth reasons." Jokes in the engineering channel turned brittle.

Jack, normally sarcastic and unbreakable, hovered near Sam's desk one afternoon, eyes tired. "I can't tell if we're winning," he said, "or just bleeding slower."

Sam didn't have an answer.

The Speed vs. Sustainability Battle

The following week, Priya returned with a roadmap aggressive enough to qualify as a cry for help.

"Three new modules this quarter," she said, clicking through mockups like a dealer flipping cards.

"Three?" Sam asked. "We don't have the capacity for one."

"We will," she said. "Hiring has already started."

"You mean re-restarted."

She waved a hand. "We're back to growth mode. We can't slow down now."

Then Colin Reeves entered the room.

Colin - ex–Big-Tech VP, crisp suit jacket, smile calibrated at a 5-degree tilt - had been parachuted in by investors as a "strategic advisor." He walked like someone who had never waited for anything.

"Speed wins," he declared within three minutes of meeting the engineering org. "Tech companies die from slowness, not mistakes."

Jonas tried diplomacy. "We need to balance sustainability"

"Balance is for accountants," Colin said. "We need velocity."

Priya nodded. Half the room nodded. Sam wanted to flip his table.

He argued: "Velocity without stability isn't speed. It's slide."

Colin grinned. "Slide fast enough, and it still counts as momentum."

Sam forced a polite smile, but something snapped inside him. He'd spent years building systems thoughtful enough to survive chaos. Colin's philosophy was gasoline poured into a dry engine.

The tension escalated.

Priya pushed for more features.

Colin pushed for more hires.

Jonas pushed for more collaboration.

The board pushed for "aggressive acceleration signals."

Sam pushed everything back.

"We can't sprint through burnout," he said in one meeting. "We're at the point where people are deleting Slack instead of messages."

Colin chuckled. "Engineers are always dramatic."

Sam drove home through rain streaking across the windshield, whispering the question he couldn't shake:

"Are we measuring the wrong things?"

It echoed louder than any dashboard.

Redefining What to Measure

The question followed Sam everywhere - into meetings, hallways, the elevator. It lingered behind every conversation about deployment frequency or sprint velocity. No number of green dashboards could drown it out.

One evening, long after most people had left, Sam walked the rows of desks in the dimmed office. The glow of the wall-mounted screens cast shimmering greens and blues across the space. It looked like a control center for a spaceship running perfectly - if you didn't account for the unseen casualties.

He stopped in front of a dashboard tracking deployment frequency. It read like a victory flag: 62 features deployed this month.

The uptime chart sat beside it, boasting 99.97%.

The error rate graph flickered near zero.

On paper, they looked impeccable.

But Sam couldn't forget the tremble in the voice of a junior engineer during a one-on-one earlier that week: "I haven't taken a day off in nine months. I'm scared things will break if I'm not here."

He couldn't forget the engineer who quietly resigned after the layoffs, leaving a note that said simply: *"I don't know what we're building anymore."*

He couldn't forget the production incident that had been triaged so quickly the dashboard never registered it - but the human cost did: two engineers up until 4am, then back online by 9am.

Those metrics measured motion, not meaning.

Sam closed his eyes. He thought of an old phrase Jonas once used: "Systems drift toward chaos unless someone steers them."

They were drifting. Silent, steady drift masked by the illusion of green charts.

The next morning, he walked into the product leadership room during a planning session. Priya was drawing an ambitious roadmap, three features deep, each tied to assumptions rather than evidence. Colin leaned over her shoulder like a coach insisting the team run faster.

Sam uncapped a marker, walked to the whiteboard, and erased the sprint-planning grid.

"Hey!" Priya protested.

Sam wrote two words in its place:

OKRs. Outcomes.

He turned to the room.

"We can't simply optimize for velocity anymore," he said. "Velocity tells us how fast we're moving. OKRs tell us which direction we should be heading."

Someone snorted; someone else murmured.

Colin leaned back. "Oh boy. A metaphor."

Sam ignored him.

"We've been measuring steps," he said. "We need to measure intention and direction. Deployment frequency tells us how often we move. It doesn't tell us whether we moved towards our target."

He drew three boxes:

Objective: Improve Reliability; Key Result: Reduce incidents by 40%

Objective: Increase User Trust; Key Result: Support satisfaction 90%+

Objective: Shorten Time to Value; Key Result: Enterprise Onboarding completed within 30 minutes

"These metrics tell us something," Sam said. "They're connected to reality, not vanity."

The room went quiet; not with resistance, but with dawning recognition.

Priya rubbed her temples. "This actually... makes sense."

Colin gave a performative shrug but said nothing.

Within two weeks, OKRs replaced velocity charts in the engineering channel. The dashboard screens didn't disappear, but their prominence dimmed. Teams started their weekly syncs with "Here's what improved for users," not "Here's what we shipped."

It wasn't a revolution.

But it was reorientation.

And suddenly, the engine felt like it had steering again.

A Different Operating Altitude: As A Director

April arrived with cherry blossoms on the sidewalks and tension in every meeting room. Investors wanted proof the company could scale responsibly after the layoffs. Product wanted speed. Engineering wanted air. Jonas wanted all of it, somehow, without becoming the villain.

One Friday afternoon he called Sam into the glass-walled conference room. The door closed softly behind them. The sunlight hit the table in narrow, golden strips - too serene for the conversation Sam expected.

Jonas slid a folder across the table.

"You're being promoted," he said. "Director of Engineering."

Sam blinked. "That feels... sudden."

"It isn't," Jonas replied. "You've been doing the job for months. You installed discipline during chaos. You pushed back on speed when it mattered. You steered us toward outcomes, not output. This is overdue."

The document inside the folder looked strangely formal - salary adjustments, expanded stock options, new responsibilities, reporting lines, expectations. Everything that once would have thrilled him now felt abstract, distant, floating several inches above where his feet actually stood.

"Congratulations," Jonas said. "You've built leaders. Now you grow + lead them."

Sam nodded, trying to decide if pride or dread sat heavier on his chest.
"I feel... farther from the music," he admitted.

Jonas smiled, something warm but weary in the expression. "Maybe your job now is to conduct it."

Later that day, Sam stood outside with Ava, the design lead, sipping tea while the city hummed below. She raised her cup.

"To the new Director," she said. "How does it feel?"

"Like gasping at high altitude," he replied. "Thinner air. Broader view. But barely any grip."

Ava smiled. "Then breathe differently, not harder."

He laughed despite himself. He hated it when Ava could so effortlessly distill complexity into clarity.

The next morning, he stepped into the office with a new sense of quiet awareness. He was no longer the person hunting memory leaks at midnight. He wasn't the one arguing over branch protection or debugging DB migrations. His vantage point had widened. And with it came a new responsibility: not to write the code, but to maintain the conditions where good code could emerge.

He wondered if this was what growing up looked like in engineering - learning to let go of the keyboard without losing the craft.

Charts Up, Hearts Down (Closing Scene)

The office lights dimmed automatically at 9 p.m., shifting from bright productivity mode to the softer glow of "night operations." Most employees were long gone. Rows of monitors blinking like distant satellites.

Sam walked slowly through the aisles, letting the quiet settle around him. The dashboards along the wall continued their pulsing rotation:

deploy counts rising, uptime stable, latency graphs hovering at comfortable lows. Everything looked healthy. Perfect, even.

Green, green, green.

He paused in front of the largest dashboard - an enormous screen showing a mosaic of metrics. The colors glowed proudly, a digital trophy case.

But in the glass reflection, he didn't see victory.

He saw exhaustion.

He saw the empty chairs of the teammates they had let go.
He saw the forced smiles in retros.
He saw the Slack channels full of silent participants.
He saw Jack's haunted expression the day he'd asked, "Are we winning... or just bleeding slower?"

Charts up.
Hearts down.

Sam closed his eyes.

He placed his hand on the edge of the dashboard - just a touch - and whispered, barely audible:

"We're not measuring what matters."

He imagined what a healthier dashboard might look like:

A graph of team burnout trending downward.

A measure of psychological safety trending upward.

A line for "engineer joy" peaking after a good refactor.

A metric for sustainable pace.

A score for clarity.

An index for meaning.

A heartbeat chart for culture.

None of these metrics existed.

But maybe they could.

The next morning, Sam drafted a memo to the engineering org:

Subject: What We Choose to Measure
Metrics matter. But meaning matters more.
Velocity describes motion.
Outcomes describe purpose.
This quarter, let's mesure both.
 - Sam

He pinned it to the engineering Slack channel. No fanfare.

Just quiet acknowledgment, like a candle lit in a dark room.

Sam shut down his laptop early that day - a rare act of rebellion - and stepped outside. The spring air felt cool against his face. The city smelled of rain and ambition. He walked slowly toward home, feeling - perhaps for the first time since Series B - that some clarity was returning.

The company would keep pushing. Investors would keep demanding. Features would keep shipping. Dashboards would keep pulsing green.

But now the team had a compass again.

And so did he.

Closing Business Snapshot

Stage	Series B -> Hypergrowth Stage
Company Value	$165 M
ARR	$20 M run-rate
Total Profit	– $8 M
Total Funding Raised	$46 million
Total Employees	150
Eng Employees	60
Sam's Equity	3% (Fully vested)
Infra Bill	$100k/month

Concept Learned: OKRs and Healthy Velocity

Sam learned that speed alone doesn't define progress. Velocity shows how fast a team moves; OKRs define why. Without alignment between the two, teams generate motion, not momentum.

Engineering dashboards once centered on DORA metrics - deploy frequency, MTTR, change failure rate - valuable signals, but incomplete. They measured activity, not purpose. Sam realized that measuring output without outcomes was like tracking heart rate without knowing whether the runner was sprinting toward a finish line or a cliff.

How Sam Influenced Objectives to Yield Business Results

He replaced the company's obsession with raw velocity charts using a balanced scorecard across three lenses:

- **Velocity** - how quickly the team delivers

- **Quality** - how reliably that work performs

- **Customer Adoption** - how customers use and pay for features

Every sprint connected features to OKRs - explicit objectives tied to user or business impact. Story points gave way to stories of improvement: incidents reduced, friction removed, onboarding shortened.

One quarter, a team shipped fewer tickets but halved their production bugs. Sam called it the company's best sprint.

Dashboards stayed, but now lived beside narrative context - brief paragraphs explaining why each metric mattered.

By year's end, the company had learned a simple truth:

Moving fast is good.

Moving well is better.

Moving with purpose is best.

Chapter 8

When the System Outgrows Your Plans

A Company Too Big to Hold

The staff no longer fit inside a single building, let alone a single mental model. It had spilled past its walls, across time zones, and into every corner of Sam's life. Three hundred and twenty people now wore the company badge - engineers in Portland, designers in Austin, PMs scattered across New York and Vancouver, engineering contractors in Bangalore and Manila, and a newly hired data science group based out of Dublin, Ireland.

Sam Desai, now Director of Engineering, sat at the center of that sprawl like a hub in a wheel that kept sprouting new spokes. Under him sat three engineering managers - Lena, steady and methodical; Jack, sarcastic but dependable; and a newcomer named Ravi, sharp but still learning the cultural rhythms. Each managed their own product domain. Each had their own challenges. Each depended on Sam for context, approval, direction, conflict mediation, and - lately - a kind of emotional glue.

His own calendar resembled a Tetris board someone had given up on. Blocks of meetings overlapped and crushed each other. Every morning began with a strategy sync. Afternoons dissolved into roadmap reviews, performance cycles, budget conversations, and "quick" check-ins that were never quick. Evenings belonged to Europe or Asia, depending on who needed him.

He couldn't remember the last time he opened an IDE.
Or started a pull request.
Or some backend Python code he didn't just skim for his own
nostalgia.

Mission statements had become as mutable as the weather - rewritten
three times since Series B, each new version arriving with a glossy
slide template and a carefully chosen inspirational verb. The OKRs
stacked beneath them like nested Russian dolls: large, ambitious
goals refined into smaller, ambiguous ones. Some were useful, others
decorative. The roadmap lived everywhere and nowhere at once -
twelve pods shipping in parallel, each sprint sprinting toward a
different horizon.

Sam wasn't fighting complexity anymore.
He was drowning in it.

Fragmented Harmony

The roadmap technically aligned with OKRs. At least, that's what the
decks claimed. The planning spreadsheets resembled a collage of
negotiations rather than a strategy. Product teams built features that
matched quarterly targets but drifted away from the original
long-term architecture. Important systems accumulated debt like
rust. Each pod optimized for its slice of the world, unaware that its
changes were another team's iceberg.

The microservice network - once Sam's pride - somehow mutated into
a distributed monolith. Each service had grown thick, opinionated,
and entangled. APIs overlapped like messy conversations.
Observability tools reported errors with the frantic energy of a
telethon hotline.

Sam kept a whiteboard in his office titled THREADS.
Blue for frontend dependencies.

Red for backend logic.
Green for database migrations.
Purple for cross-pod communication.

The lines had become so dense that the board resembled a topographical map of anxiety. When he updated it, he felt like a surgeon drawing incisions on a patient too fragile to operate on.

Career ladders had become formal PDFs - dense with verbs like *inspire, align, influence*. Coaching had once been spontaneous conversations around whiteboards; now it was a recurring block on the calendar, part of a system of rubrics and performance ratings. Retrospectives felt less like learning and more like rituals. People nodded politely, thanked each other for "transparency," and then quietly changed nothing.

Still, Sam fought to maintain some kind of soul.

Every Friday, he sent out an email titled Friday Threads, a small collection of notes - wins, lessons, moments of humility. At first the replies were paragraphs; gratitude mixed with camaraderie. Then they became sentences. Then emojis.

Then silence.

The silence unnerved him more than any outage or security breach.

The Confrontation That Broke the Room

It happened during a cross-team design review, the kind where half the attendees turned off cameras to multitask and the other half stayed on mute to avoid appearing confrontational.

Nikhil Singh, a bright young engineer from a top graduate program, had prepared a thorough proposal to rewrite the analytics pipeline.

His slides were crisp. His tone was impatient. His ambition outpaced his diplomacy.

When he finished presenting, Sam asked a handful of clarifying questions about scope, migration steps, and risk.

Nikhil exhaled sharply, a tiny gesture amplified by the microphone. "With respect, we move too slow," he said.

The room stilled.

"Half these dependencies are political, not technical," Nikhil continued. "We spend more time debating than building."

Jack, sitting in the corner of the room with his laptop open like a shield, gave a humorless chuckle.
"He's not wrong," Jack said. "We're drowning in meetings. People want to ship, not justify and they don't want to take orders from those out of touch with the codebase"

The words landed with more force than criticism. They sounded like they were in grief.

Sam looked down at the conference table, at the blurry reflection of fluorescent lights trembling on its surface. He felt the weight of every lost hour, every meeting where he'd nodded through his own exhaustion, every moment where leadership meant abstraction instead of creation.

"You're right," Sam said quietly. "I don't code anymore."

Nikhil looked startled, unsure if Sam was agreeing or confessing.

"My job now isn't to write code," Sam continued. "It's to make sure you all can with joy and purpose."

A silence followed - heavy, unsure.

"I didn't mean.... " Nikhil began.

"It's fine," Sam said gently. "Keep pushing. You're supposed to push. Just remember - when you lead, you'll feel this distance too."

After the meeting, the hallway reeked of unsaid things. Sam closed the door to his office, opened his notebook, and wrote:

Distance is not failure; it's altitude.
He stared at it, then crossed it out.

Politics as Architecture

Leadership syncs began to feel like geopolitical summits - teeth-grindingly polite, strategically evasive, and full of charts used as weapons.

Each department defended its metrics like territory.
Priya argued for doubling feature output.
Jonas warned about quality regressions.
The ops team showed alarming cloud-cost graphs.

Amira, the Operations Lead, delivered a slide showing AWS expenses ballooning toward two hundred thousand dollars a month.

"We're optimizing for reckless speed," she said. "Not thoughtful efficiency."

Colin Reeves - the advisor investors had parachuted in - leaned back in his chair with a confident smile. He had the air of someone who mistook previous luck for permanent superiority. His silver hair caught the overhead lights like a halo he'd awarded himself.

"Efficiency doesn't raise valuations," he said. "Velocity does."

Sam clenched his pen. He wanted to argue that velocity built on fragility collapses faster - but the meeting moved on, swallowing his protest like a wave swallowing a rock.

When it ended, Amira caught up with him near the kitchen.

"You looked like you wanted to say something," she said.

"I wanted to scream," Sam admitted.

"Coffee?"

They escaped to the small corner café across the parking lot, sliding into a booth that finally insulated them from the noise. Rain began tapping the windows in slow patterns.

"You know what this feels like?" Sam said, wrapping both hands around his mug. "Upgrading a plane while flying it."

Amira raised an eyebrow. "Go on."

"You can't land. You can't pause. You bolt new wings mid-air, reinforce the old ones, and pray the engines hold. Every new piece adds lift and adds weight."

She let out a slow breath. "That explains the turbulence."

"It's not bad intentions," Sam said. "Everyone is holding their pieces together. But the more parts we add, the more we lose aerodynamic integrity."

Amira nodded, tracing a finger along the rim of her cup.
"We're scaling faster than we're learning."

They sat in silence, understanding something that wouldn't fit into any dashboard.

The Slow Erosion

March arrived, and with it came the first COVID warnings. Within weeks the office emptied. Chairs remained but people evaporated into Zoom windows. Slack channels turned into lifelines. The company tried to simulate culture with virtual coffee chats and meme threads. For a while, it almost worked.

Then came the slow erosion.

Zoom fatigue hit them all like a slow toxin.
Time zones multiplied into a nightmare.
Every meeting started sounding like an echo.
Every voice felt distant.
Every calendar alert felt like a gut-punch.

Sam's days stretched into marathons. Europe at dawn. East Coast mid-morning. West Coast late afternoon. Asia-based contractors at night. His laptop became an extension of his hands. His coffee machine became his only colleague with consistent availability.

He joked about time zones eating his soul, but the joke began sounding too true.

Retrospectives devolved into polite acknowledgments.
Demos lost their energy.
Friday donuts disappeared, replaced by emojis shaped like donuts.

One evening, long after he'd promised himself, he would log off at a reasonable hour, a Slack DM blinked from Priya:

Don't lose yourself in the system.

No context. No follow-up. No emoji.

Sam stared at it for a long time.
He wanted to reply: *Too late?*
But he typed nothing.

Later, he reopened GitHub, hoping code might anchor him. The syntax felt foreign, like a language he once devoured but no longer spoke. He closed the tab and felt the loss like a missing limb.

The Winter of Deep Cuts

By summer, whispers began circulating again - budget tightening, revenue projections slipping, experiments failing quietly. Productivity looked steady, but morale sagged. A team that once thrived on momentum now moved as if pulling a heavy rope behind them.

Jonas scheduled a leadership call with cameras off - a bad sign.

"We're doing another round," he said. "Finance says twenty percent this time."

The air left Sam's lungs.
He knew the math.
He knew the script.
He hated both.

"Who delivers the news to engineering?" he asked.

"You," Jonas said quietly. "You are the best proxy of our Leadership. We trust you."

Trust in that moment felt like a huge burden.

Monday morning, three hundred faces appeared in a single Zoom grid - floating squares, anxious eyes, stiff shoulders, digital silhouettes. Some believed it was a routine quarterly update. Others braced for impact.

Sam swallowed once, twice, then spoke.

"This is the hardest announcement I've had to make. The market has shifted, and we need to reduce our team size."

A few gasped. Several cameras blinked off. One person muted themselves so quickly their hand blurred.

"This is not about performance," he continued, hearing himself recite a language he despised. "It's about sustainability."

He talked until the silence felt unbearable, then ended the call.

Afterward, he scrolled through Slack - messages of gratitude, shock, anger, resignation. He answered none.

When he finally left the office, rain streaked down the empty streets. The city looked hollowed out. Sam walked instead of driving, letting the quiet fill him.

At home, he sat by the window, opened his notebook, and wrote:

Systems are meant to serve people. Somewhere along the way, ours learned to serve itself.

He closed the book and let the city hum around him.

The Architecture Reveals Your Org (i.e. Conway's Law)

It happened weeks later, during an architecture review. Sam traced a request path across seven services. Each hop represented a team handoff - backend to data, data to analytics, analytics to ML ops, ML ops back to backend, then finally frontend.

Seven teams.
Seven borders.
Seven opportunities for misalignment.

The service graph looked familiar. Too familiar.

It looked like the org chart.

Then it hit him.

The system wasn't broken.
It was autobiographical.

Conway's Law: the idea that systems reflect the communication structures of the teams that build them - wasn't theoretical anymore. It explained the last 18 months of his life.

If a service was brittle, the team building it was stretched thin.
If a workflow required six approvals, the org was built on hierarchy.
If integrations constantly broke, communication constantly broke.
If microservices behaved like silos, teams behaved like silos.

Sam had spent two years debugging code.
But the bugs weren't technical.
They were sociological.

Once he saw it, he couldn't unsee it.

How Sam Fought Back

He didn't add more rules.
He removed boundaries.

He created cross-functional design reviews instead of escalations.
He wrote "interface contracts" between teams - lightweight agreements of how they should collaborate rather than bureaucratic fences.
He reorganized pods around the flow of work instead of reporting lines.
He paired engineers across distant teams during incidents, breaking silos with empathy.
He standardized deployment pipelines across orgs - not for aesthetics but to force shared habits.
He revived retros as "topology repair meetings," asking one new question:

Where did the communication break?

Slowly, architecture and organization began aligning again - not because Sam dictated it, but because he removed the surfaces where they conflicted.

He realized engineering wasn't about code or systems or deploys.

It was about communication patterns made physical.

Closing Business Snapshot

Stage	Late Series B → Series C
Company Value	$300 M (Valuation)
ARR	$65 M
Annual Profit	– $15 M
Total Funding Raised	$46 million
Total Employees	300
Eng Employees	120
Sam's Equity	2.8% (Fully vested)
Infra Bill	$225k/month

Concept Learned: Conway's Law Rediscovered

Sam learned the truth behind one of engineering's most cited but least understood principles:
Conway's Law - *systems mirror the communication patterns of the teams that build them.*

In theory, it sounds like an architectural constraint.
In practice, it explained the last eighteen months of his life.

As the company grew past two hundred people, the organization chart had quietly become the architecture diagram. The new microservices weren't micro; they were silos. Each team built its own stack, its own tools, its own timelines. Integrations weren't failing because of code - they were failing because of communication boundaries.

If a service was brittle, it was because the team responsible was stretched thin.
If a service was over-engineered, it was because the team was insecure.
If a workflow took six meetings to approve, the architecture mimicked the same path.

The system wasn't failing.
It was doing exactly what the org structure had taught it to do.

This realization hit Sam during a late-night architecture review when he traced a request path across seven services. Seven. Each hop represented a team handoff, a Slack message, a meeting that should've been an email, or sometimes, radio silence.

The distributed monolith wasn't accidental.
It was autobiographical.

How Sam Celebrated Conway's Law

He began mapping system failures back to communication failures.
Every incident review included a new question:
"Who had to talk to whom for this to work?"

Patterns emerged.
Bugs weren't technical; they were sociological.
The teams building the product didn't communicate the way the product needed to behave.

So, Sam acted - not with more rules, but with fewer boundaries.

He pushed cross-functional design reviews where engineers, designers, PMs, and SREs *sat together* instead of escalating across ladder rungs.

He created "interface contracts" between teams as lightweight agreements, not bureaucratic fences.

He reorganized pods around the flow of work rather than reporting lines.

He softened the edges between groups by pairing engineers from distant teams during incidents.

He revived retros, not as complaint sessions, but as topology repair meetings: "Where did the communication break?"

He fought hard to standardize deployment pipelines across orgs - not for aesthetics, but to force shared habits.

Slowly, the architecture and the org chart started aligning again - not because Sam dictated it, but because he removed the surfaces where they conflicted.

That was the real lesson:
Organizational design is architecture.

Architecture is organizational design.

And if you don't shape the communication pathways early, your systems will do it for you - permanently.

Chapter 9

Leadership From a Distance

Remote Overnight

The email arrived on a Sunday evening in March 2020, the kind of email that would normally follow a long discussion, a leadership meeting, or at least a paragraph of explanation. But this one offered nothing - just one line, sent at 7:42 p.m.:

Effective immediately - we are remote until further notice.

No rationale. No horizon. No promise.

By Monday morning, the office was a mausoleum. Desks abandoned mid-task. Coffee mugs left half-full. A few succulents sat on windowsills like tiny green survivors, unaware their owners weren't coming back.

Sam stood in the doorway long enough for the motion sensors to decide he wasn't real. The lights clicked off, plunging the room into a soft gray darkness.

That evening, he set up his new "office" between a pile of laundry and a stack of notebooks. He stacked books under the laptop to look less like a hostage on Zoom. The first invite landed at 6:15 a.m. He wasn't fully awake until the fourth meeting, by which point he'd already forgotten what time meant.

When he caught his own reflected face on Zoom - over lit, slightly haunted - he looked like someone mid-confession.

He wasn't alone. Everyone looked like that.

This was the new reality; a transition made without ceremony. It felt less like a shift and more like a door slamming shut.

Slack Overload

Slack had always been noisy, but now it felt like a malfunctioning fire alarm. New channels spawned hourly:
#covid-updates,
#remote-hacks,
#kids-on-calls,
#mental-health,
#random-cry-for-help,
and, tragically, #furlough-support.

Half the posts were frantic. Half were jokes trying to mask the frantic. An engineer uploaded a photo of his dog with the caption "my new intern." Someone else posted that their spouse had been furloughed that morning. Emojis piled on: hearts, tears, and the new favorite, :scream-cat:.

The roadmap disintegrated overnight. Clients froze budgets. Investors paused conversations. One of the OKRs for the quarter was rewritten simply as:

Keep the lights on.

Sam watched the roadmap on ProductBoard like a doctor watching an EKG. The pulse was faint, erratic. Every time someone moved a card into "In Progress," another person dragged something into "Blocked."

Chaos wasn't new to Sam. What was new was the stillness beneath it - everyone working alone, in quiet rooms scattered across the country.

There was no shoulder-tap. No hallway collision. No chance to see panic in someone's eyes and say, "Let's breathe for a minute."

There was only text on screens, too much and never enough.

Time zone Drift

The company had gone global before it had gone prepared.

They brought on contractors in Europe, India, and South America to solve bandwidth issues caused by the pandemic. Overnight, meetings stretched like melted taffy across time zones. Sam found himself joining calls at 3 a.m., then forgetting breakfast, then answering a Slack thread at midnight because it was morning somewhere.

His new greeting became:

"Good morning, afternoon or evening - whichever applies."

Amira joked that they had entered "permanent jet lag without any travel photos." She was right. People's voices sounded flattened by delay, like everyone was speaking through cloth.

One afternoon, Sam logged into a meeting and saw twelve faces in twelve rectangles, each one tinted by a different type of exhaustion. Someone's kid cried in the background. Someone else's partner vacuumed loudly. A cat walked across a keyboard. One engineer whispered, "Sorry, my landlord is fixing the boiler."

Every moment felt frayed. Even bandwidth felt emotional.

They were a distributed system now - one with too many hops, too many dropped packets, and latency that couldn't be measured on any dashboard.

The Resilience Debate

The layoffs returned in June - another round of euphemisms, another wave of scripts from HR that felt like theatre.

The spreadsheet with names looked like a battlefield list. Sam hated the columns: "Tenure," "Comp," "Impact Score," "Role Criticality." As if humanity could be filtered by formulas.

He spent nearly five hours straight on termination calls. One engineer muted his microphone to sob. Another tried to smile, saying, "Thanks for fighting for us. I know this wasn't you." That one nearly broke him.

After the final call, he closed his laptop and let the ghost image of the screen fade on its own. Outside, the street was empty - like even the city had been laid off.

The next morning Priya called an emergency leadership sync. Her voice came through the speaker raw, brittle.

"We can't just keep cutting," she said. "What's the actual vision?"

"Survival," Jonas answered.

"Survival is not a vision," she shot back.

Amira added, "People are terrified. They need leaders, not charts."

Then Colin Reeves, who somehow still had an advisor badge despite contributing nothing but cynicism, muttered:

"Fear's a great motivator."

Sam's jaw clenched. "Fear is a short-term motivator," he said. "It burns fuel we don't have."

Silence.

Priya leaned forward. "Then what do we build on?"

Sam opened a digital whiteboard and quickly drew a simple cluster diagram.

"In code," he said, "resilience means the system doesn't die if one server fails. You build redundancy, failover paths, healthy defaults."

He paused.

"For people, resilience is the same. If one person burns out, the whole team shouldn't crash."

For a moment, everyone was quiet. Even Colin.

Amira finally whispered, "That's the first thing today that made sense."

Life Inside the Collapse

They experimented with tiny morale hacks:
#gratitude channels, no-meeting Fridays, optional mental-health hours, random "anyone want to talk about anything that isn't work?" rooms.

A few engineers shared pictures of home-cooked meals. Someone posted a sunrise. Someone posted a meme that read: *What day is it? Yes.*

It wasn't enough. But it was something.

By August, the world outside had dissolved into sirens, masks, and empty streets. Inside, the company slipped into its own form of fever dream.

Workdays were blurred. Weekends vanished. Sam woke at 3 a.m., checked Slack, scrolled through notifications like a doctor triaging a ward.

He tried meditation apps. He tried warm milk. He tried reading. None of it stopped his brain from replaying difficult conversations.

Every Thursday the leadership team met. The agenda never changed: finances, burn rate, "strategic adjustments." Sam watched the fatigue spread. Priya's voice lost its lift. Jonas's eyes lost their light. Amira coughed through muted audio.

The company still deployed code, but no one celebrated. They released features with the same energy hospitals issue discharge paperwork - routine, necessary, devoid of joy.

The city outside his window was a ghost. Inside, he felt like one too.

Sam's Breaking Point

The second pandemic wave hit harder than the first. Clients folded. Investors insisted on deeper cuts. HR circulated a new script: softer wording, sharper consequences.

Layoffs happened over Zoom - silent disappearances as cameras winked out. No goodbyes. No shared room. No catharsis.

After the final conversation, Sam stared at his own reflection on the black screen.

"This isn't what I signed up for," he whispered.

He wasn't sure whether he said it aloud or thought it so loudly it felt spoken.

He started measuring a new secret metric in a private spreadsheet:

Human Downtime.
Resignations. Sick leave. Unexplained delays. Slack messages ending with "just tired."

The graph climbed faster than revenue ever had.

Then came the call from Priya.

"I'm leaving," she said.

"Leaving the company?"

"Leaving the grind."

He didn't try to keep her. He only said, "I get it."

"You should think about it too," she whispered. "Before it eats you alive."

He stared at his ceiling for hours after the call ended.

Some decisions don't require courage. Only timing.

A Quiet Breakdown

Amira invited him to a small Friday group of managers called the "Resilience Roundtable" - a place to vent, cry, or simply exist. Cameras off. No recording. No metrics.

One project manager from London said, "I wish humans had restarts. Like servers. Just shut down, clear memory leaks, reboot."

Sam answered softly, "That's what this group is - a soft reboot."

It wasn't much. But it kept a few people from breaking.

Ava, now at another startup, emailed him one night:

Design is about constraints. Leadership is too.
Sometimes the constraint is your own health.

He reread it twice. Typed a reply. Deleted it.

Sleep fled entirely. He woke automatically at 3 a.m., refreshing dashboards that meant nothing. His brain still believed green checkmarks equaled safety.

One morning, at 4:07 a.m., he wrote into his journal:

Maybe resilience isn't bouncing back.

Maybe it's learning where not to break again.

The sunrise made the ink look faint, almost erased.

Then came the next restructuring. Fewer employees. Fewer hopes. Fewer illusions.

He went through the motions, but his soul felt unplugged.

That evening he sat by the window and watched snow dust the city. In the quiet, he felt the smallest flicker of something he hadn't felt in months:

Clarity.

Not hope. Not strength.

Just clarity.

He wasn't sure he wanted this life anymore. And clarity, he realized, was the first step toward any exit.

Closing Business Snapshot

Stage	Series C - Pandemic Stage
Company Value	$750 M
ARR	$60 M
Annual Profit	- $25 M
Total Funding Raised	$106 million
Total Employees	240
Eng Employees	100
Sam's Equity	2.6% (vested)
Infra Bill	$250k/month

Concept Learned: Managing a Globally Distributed Org

Sam learned that remote leadership wasn't an extension of management - it was a complete redesign.
Before COVID, alignment came from proximity: hallway conversations, whiteboard collisions, the ambient rhythm of a team breathing the same office air.

Then the world shut down.

Suddenly, silence wasn't calm - it was ambiguity.
Slack channels went quiet for hours, then exploded without warning.
Decisions evaporated inside private messages.
Meetings multiplied, but clarity did not.

The system's throughput stalled, not from lack of talent, but from lack of signal strength.

Remote work exposed a law Sam had never articulated:
Alignment doesn't die from disagreement. It dies from silence.

Distributed teams didn't drift because people were wrong - they drifted because nobody noticed the drift until it was too late. The architecture began fracturing the same way the people did: endpoints timing out, messages dropped, retries stacking up.

He realized that leading remotely required a different sensory system.
Managers in an office read the room.
Remote leaders read the *delay*.
A long pause before joining Zoom.
A Slack message edited three times.
A stand-up update that sounded too rehearsed.
A camera that stayed off a little too often.

These were not performance issues - they were latency issues.

Sam learned to treat remote work the way SREs treated distributed systems: diagnose the blind spots, shorten the communication hops, reduce the noise, strengthen the signal.

How Sam Time-traveled With Global Teams

He rebuilt communication not around status updates but around throughput clarity.

He replaced oversized meetings with structured async updates - short, predictable, timestamped.
He scheduled "open windows" instead of standing meetings, where anyone could drop in for five minutes without booking a slot.
He introduced *"heartbeat messages,"* lightweight check-ins that

asked, "What feels unclear this week?"
He taught managers that remote trust wasn't built by visibility - it was built by responsiveness.

He also set a rule for himself:
If he sensed someone going dark, he assumed "overload," not "lack of commitment."
It transformed how he coached.
Not "Why didn't you update this?"
But "What signal did you need that you didn't get?"

When layoffs returned, he delivered them with the only remote leadership tool that mattered: presence. Camera on, voice steady, no euphemisms, no shortcuts.

Even then, the silence afterward felt heavier than the decision.

By the end of the "chapter", Sam understood the truth about distributed leadership:

You can't control people remotely.

You can only strengthen the signal, so they move with clarity and context, not fear.

And when the system is falling apart, silence is the real outage.

Chapter 10

IPO Dreams, IPO Nightmares

The Glow of Going Public

From the outside, the new headquarters looked like a building that had already been successful for decades - steel-framed glass, humongous etched signage near the entrance, and a lobby paved in marble so polished that it reflected the ceiling lights like a still lake. It was designed to signal permanence, wealth, and inevitability. *We belong with the giants*, it proclaimed. Inside, posters stretched across the walls: *We're Going Public! One Team, One Mission. IPO 202X.* Each slogan carried the breathless confidence of a company convinced of its destiny.

But beneath that glossy surface, Sam Desai felt a strange dissonance. He had never cared for symbols, and now he was surrounded by them - (aspirational) stock tickers mounted above coffee stations, giant countdown clocks for the roadshow, monitors in the hallways looping clips of smiling executives and customer testimonials. It was surreal, almost theatrical, as if the company were rehearsing for a play.

Being VP of Engineering was supposed to feel like a peak - something earned, something triumphant. Instead, it felt like stepping into a role scripted for a higher being than himself. He had traded his hoodie for a blazer, not because he wanted to, but because a banker had offhandedly mentioned that "institutional investors respond better" to formal attire. His days had become a blur of long meetings - board prep, audit prep, legal prep, anything prep - and his nights dissolved into endless document reviews and emails marked urgent by people who had never shipped a line of code.

Eight years earlier, everything had been simpler. He had sat in a cramped coworking space debugging a failing upload parser while a space heater rattled beside him. If something broke, he fixed it. If customers struggled, he talked to them. The work was messy but honest. Now the work was polished but hollow. He was still in the same company, technically, but the company he had loved felt like a faded photograph.

Even the air felt different: filtered, temperature-controlled, perfumed with the faint scent of new carpet. The CEO called it "an environment of confidence." Sam privately nicknamed it "the smell of money and fear."

When Investor Decks Become the Roadmap

In the months leading to the IPO, the product roadmap underwent an evolution that made Sam visibly uneasy. It no longer originated in user interviews, community feedback, or the engineering team's long-term strategy. It shamelessly originated straight from the investor deck - a thirty-slide narrative designed to make analysts nod in approvals during the roadshow.

Features weren't prioritized by value anymore; they were prioritized by optics. A seamless onboarding redesign mattered because it photographed well. A machine-learning enhancement mattered because it impressed institutional buyers. A major architectural refactor that would reduce downtime by 40% mattered far less - no banker asked about it, and no amount of powerpoint magic could dramatize it enough.

The engineers joked that Jira had become a screenplay. "Act I: Innovation. Act II: Compliance. Act III: Despair," Jack had muttered months before he quit. It was funny then. Now it felt prophetic.

Every time Sam questioned the logic of deprioritizing crucial technical work in favor of surface-level improvements, Finance replied with robotic precision: *"Those are post-IPO problems."*
post-IPO problems. The phrase felt like a glitch in the system. It suggested that time could be borrowed indefinitely from the future without consequence. It also had this nagging implication that the future was someone else's problem.

Sam could feel the architecture groaning. Technical debt had become institutional debt. The once-elegant microservice network had grown into a cluster of brittle, overextended modules - a distributed monolith in the shape of an org chart. But anything not directly tied to the IPO narrative was quietly deferred into a folder called "Q+1," which everyone understood meant "never."

He still tried to fight for the right things, but each attempt was met with glossy explanations about "market readiness," "investor optics," and "perceived execution momentum." Sam had spent his whole career building products grounded in real-world use. Now he was building a story - the kind with a good soundtrack and weak engineering.

And it was exhausting.

Politics at Scale

As the company ballooned past a thousand employees, politics became not just an undercurrent but a structural reality. With more people came more narratives, more agendas, more invisible currents. What used to be a team of builders now resembled a coalition of departments with overlapping mandates and competing KPIs.

Promotion season felt like election season. Some managers formed alliances, others campaigned for their people through carefully worded performance packets. The engineering floor buzzed with whispered predictions - who would rise, who would be passed over, who was quietly being sidelined. The innocence of early-stage ambition was long gone.

Priya, once the embodiment of pragmatic optimism, constantly joked that she spent more time managing perception than product. The humor was thinning, though. She had survived two layoffs, three reorganizations, and four different leadership philosophies, each one painted as a strategic pivot.

Sam noticed that even Jack - the last holdout of irreverent authenticity - seemed drained. In one one-on-one shortly before he resigned, Jack stared at his keyboard and said, "We used to build things. Now we're just filing tickets in a bureaucracy that calls itself agile." Sam tried to find the right words, but everything felt hollow and rehearsed.

He himself now spent mornings completing compliance attestations for systems he hadn't touched in years, afternoons preparing leadership decks, and evenings reviewing scripts for communication rollouts. He no longer measured his days by what he built, but by how many people he reassured.

Sometimes he wondered if he was still an engineering leader, or just a translator in a never-ending corporate relay.

The Breaking Points Continued

The first visible crack came during an IPO prep session with the CFO, Mira Patel. It was meant to be a final rehearsal for the narrative they would present to analysts: growth potential, market penetration, operational excellence. Everyone spoke in sound bites. Every sentence had been polished, scrubbed clean of uncertainty.

Priya was unusually quiet. As Mira walked through a slide showing the "Innovation Pipeline," something in her broke. She unmuted her microphone and said, with unnerving calm, "This isn't product vision anymore. This is performance theater."

The virtual room froze. Jonas tried to intervene, but she continued, "We are rehearsing confidence instead of building value. We've replaced actual user feedback with investor feedback."

Colin, the advisor whose confidence was inversely proportional to his relevance, laughed. "Optics matter more than features now. Welcome to the big leagues."

Priya didn't flinch. She closed her laptop with a decisive thud. "Then I'm not interested in these leagues."

She left the call, and for the first time in weeks, Sam felt a strange combination of dread and admiration.

Two days later, Jack sent his now-infamous resignation email. Three lines. No explanation, no justification. Sam forwarded it to HR and stared at the sent message with a sense of personal failure. He knew Jack wasn't just quitting the job; he was quitting the version of the company that no longer deserved him.

After that, the emotional fabric of the engineering team began to tear. People worked, but not with conviction. The spark had dimmed, and Sam felt partially responsible. He was a leader, after all. And leaders carry the weight of both success and disillusionment.

The State of the Engineering Union

A week later, engineering leaders asked Sam to host a town hall. They needed clarity. They needed something that wasn't another corporate celebration or a diluted reassurance. They needed truth.

Sam entered the Zoom call and saw faces - old colleagues, wide-eyed interns, new hires who had never known the messy, lovable chaos of the early years. They looked tired and uncertain, but not hopeless.

He spoke without slides at first. "You've probably heard phrases like 'engineering excellence' and 'organizational maturity,' but I want to unpack what those actually mean."

Then he pulled up a blank digital whiteboard and began to draw.

"Here is our Engineering State of the Union," he said, sketching four columns.

People & Leadership Maturity - "How we grow leaders. How we resolve problems with empathy. This is culture written in code."
Engineering Excellence - "Testing. Observability. Debt. This is the foundation we build on."
Engineering Strategy & Innovation - "Whether we still make space for curiosity, experiments, and invention."
Execution & Delivery Health - "Velocity, quality, predictability. How we ship."

"These four together measure who we are - not who the market wants us to pretend to be."

Someone asked, "Is this what the board wants?"

Sam smiled faintly. "It's what we *need*."

For the first time in months, he saw nods that weren't performative. He saw understanding. He saw relief.

For a moment, he remembered why he had stayed so long. Because building teams - real teams - still mattered to him.

Compliance as a Way of Life

But the momentum from that town hall quickly collided with the tidal wave of IPO preparation. Compliance became the ruling philosophy of the company. Auditors circulated through every workflow like an invasive species. Sarbanes–Oxley made engineering crawl at the speed of paperwork.

Pull requests now required multi-step signoffs. Deployment pipelines paused for review cycles. Slack messages were archived as potential legal fodder. Engineers joked that they should start every message with "This statement is not forward-looking," and every joke now had a warning label.

The word *risk* replaced the word *experiment* in most conversations. Innovation became something discussed nostalgically, like an old hobby everyone once enjoyed before responsibilities intervened.

Sam tried to shield the team from the worst of it, but even he couldn't escape the gravitational pull of bureaucracy. He sat in long meetings with lawyers correcting his phrasing and bankers advising him on tone. He learned which words could trigger compliance concerns. The list grew longer each week.

Sometimes, after a long day, he scrolled through old pull requests where he and Jack had debated abstractions, discussed architecture, and designed systems. Those comments felt like artifacts from a different lifetime. Now, his contributions lived in risk registers and governance matrices - long spreadsheets cataloging everything that could go wrong. He felt like he was slowly being replaced by a legal disclaimer.

The Hollow Triumph

The night before the IPO, the executive team rehearsed one last time. Photographers staged "candid team shots," complete with choreographed laughter. Bankers reviewed talking points with artificial intensity. The CEO practiced his speech in front of a mirror. The CFO refined her smile.

Sam practiced staying awake.

He still believed in the mission - somewhere under the layers of forms and filings - but the distance between belief and execution had grown wide and dangerous. He wondered if the company's growth had outpaced its soul.

And yet the next morning, IPO day unfolded like a fairy tale. The company logo glowed across stock exchange monitors. Cameras flashed. Confetti flew. People hugged, cried, and toasted. Tickers lit the atrium with green numbers, each uptick punctuated with cheers.

Sam stood among them, clapping, smiling, trying to feel what everyone else felt. But inside, a foggy stillness had settled over him. He watched the CEO ring the bell and felt admiration, pride... and a quiet grief. This was a victory. This was the moment so many had dreamed of. And yet, it felt strangely separate from the journey that had brought him here.

He thought of his old metaphor:
Startups are garage bands. IPO is the stadium tour - same music, bigger crowd.
But looking around, listening to the roar of celebration, he realized

the music wasn't the same. Somewhere along the way, someone had rewritten the lyrics.

Still, he couldn't ignore what this moment unlocked. The product and engineering teams would finally have a real runway, not just in pitch decks but in budget lines. More SREs to keep the lights on, more time to pay down the debt they'd been duct-taping for years, more freedom to make the system as stable, scalable, and secure as they'd always promised it could be.

And for his own team, the early engineers who had slept on office couches and debugged in airport lounges, this was a life-altering event. The stock grants, once theoretical numbers in a dusty HR portal, now meant mortgages paid off, college funds topped up, options that didn't exist yesterday. Sam's family would probably never have to panic over a surprise bill again. Whatever else changed, he helped build something that could now take care of dozens.

Closing Business Snapshot

Stage	Initial Public Offering
Company Value	$2.2 B (post IPO)
ARR	$145 M run-rate
Annual Profit	- $22 M
Total Funding Raised	$106 million
Total Employees	1000+
Eng Employees	~300
Sam's Equity	2.6% (Fully vested)
Infra Bill	$500k/month

Concept Learned: State of the Engineering Union

As the company marched toward its IPO, Sam learned that engineering was no longer defined by commits, roadmaps, or architecture diagrams.

It was defined by narrative clarity - the ability to measure a sprawling, uneven, sometimes fragile organization in a way that executives, auditors, and investors could understand.

The "State of the Engineering Union" began as a PowerPoint request from the CFO - "a simple overview for the bankers" - but Sam immediately knew that wasn't what it needed to be.

Slides weren't the point.
Measurement & clarity was.

Engineering maturity had to be made visible.
Not to flatter the board, but to prevent the company from breaking under the weight of its own promises.

So Sam reframed the task:

The State of the Union wasn't a deck; it was a mirror.
A way to reveal the true shape of an engineering organization - a shape everyone had felt but nobody had named.

He learned that companies often believe engineering is a cost center until the moment it fails. Then, suddenly, engineering becomes "critical infrastructure."

The State of the Union existed to prevent that amnesia.

It captured the operational truth beneath the IPO theater:

- which systems were brittle
- which processes were ceremonial
- which teams were carrying the emotional load
- which leaders were burning out quietly
- which goals were illusions

Sam discovered that what you choose to measure defines what you choose to protect.

And most executives had been protecting the wrong things.

For the first time, Sam saw engineering not as craft or execution, but as governance - a disciplined way of keeping the organization aligned with reality, not aspiration.

How Sam Addressed (Engineering) State of the Union

He built the State of the Engineering Union like an engineer, not a politician.

He decomposed the entire organization into measurable domains: People, Leadership, Velocity, Quality, Reliability, Innovation, Culture, Architecture, and Risk.

He paired every metric with a story, every number with a context, every dashboard with a truth executives couldn't ignore.

He refused to round up.

He refused to hide systemic issues behind averages.

He reported brittle systems as brittle, even when it made the CTO uncomfortable.

He documented burnout indicators as carefully as uptime.

He treated the report as a periodic refactor of the company's self-perception.

And something unusual happened:

- Teams started using the vocabulary.
- Directors referenced the metrics in planning.
- Engineers pushed back on unreasonable timelines with maturity data instead of emotion.
- Executives asked smarter questions.
- The system became more honest - slowly, unevenly, but undeniably.

On IPO day, as champagne sprayed and stock tickers scrolled across plasma screens, Sam realized the real achievement wasn't the valuation or the headlines.

It was that the engineering organization had become legible - to itself, to leadership, and to its future.

The State of the Engineering Union had made complexity measurable, and measurement had made it real.

And sometimes, Sam thought, that's the closest engineering gets to truth.

Chapter 11

After the Bell: Learning to Breathe Again

The Quiet Reset

The emails slowed first, then stopped altogether. The Slack icon turned gray. Sam deleted the calendar app from his phone and stared at the blank home screen, oddly startled by its emptiness. After a decade of meetings, launches, audits, crises, and ceremonies disguised as decisions, the absence of noise felt like stepping out of a wind tunnel.

He had promised himself six months - no board decks, no investor updates, no hiring plans, no quarterly narratives. Only space. Only air.

Austin was warmer than he remembered, a city that felt both lived-in and effortless. He rented a small house tucked near the greenbelt, where cicadas sang louder than traffic and morning air smelled faintly of cedar and soil. For the first time in years, his days had no agenda. He made coffee slowly, savoring each step instead of gulping caffeine between deadlines. He read novels instead of briefs, walked the same trail until he knew its bends by color and texture, and let silence replace strategy for the first time in a decade.

Sometimes he hiked with his family, letting his dogs and kids race ahead on the rocky path. Sometimes he walked alone, listening to the rustle of oak leaves and his own breath.

Three weeks into the sabbatical, he stopped checking LinkedIn entirely. The IPO headlines had already disappeared, replaced by new companies chasing the same bell. He felt no envy - only distance, as though he had quietly stepped out of a speeding train and watched it vanish beyond the horizon.

An Inventory of Threads

One afternoon he carried his notebook to the riverbank and sat on a sun-warmed ledge. The water murmured softly over stones, unhurried, unconcerned with velocity or metrics. Sam flipped open to a blank page and drew a single line down the center. At the top he wrote Steel Threads.

On the left side he wrote the things he had built:

- Teams. Mentorship. Systems that mostly held. Moments of clarity. Hard decisions made cleanly.

On the right side, he wrote the things that had broken:

- Sleep. Curiosity. Joy. His sense of proportion. The part of himself that believed simplicity was not naïve but necessary.

He stared at the list until the ink bled slightly, spreading at the edges like water finding cracks. His original "steel thread" metaphor - one small, strong, end-to-end story that carried a product from idea to impact - suddenly seemed fragile. Steel rusted too, he realized, when pulled too tightly for too long and never allowed to rest.

The company had grown from five people in a dusty coworking corner to more than a thousand employees spread across a dozen countries and time zones. He had grown from an anxious engineer to a VP rehearsing line for bankers. But somewhere between the early magic and the late-stage machinery, he had stopped asking the question that once defined his ambition:

What problem am I solving?

The answer used to be simple: help people build good things, quickly and cleanly. Now he wasn't sure. The notebook closed with a soft thud, as if saving the question for later.

Unlearning Velocity

As the weeks unfolded, he found himself drawn back to small acts of creation, almost shyly at first. He spun up a cheap cloud instance and wrote a few lines of Python - nothing ambitious, just enough to test whether the muscle memory still lived in him. It did. The terminal blur of commands felt like slipping into a familiar language he'd once spoken fluently.

No approvals. No compliance attestations. No legal reviews. No "material risk assessments."

Just code.

He built a tiny API one morning, then deleted it that afternoon, delighted by the freedom to treat work as play again. He remembered why the original steel thread had mattered - not because it was efficient, but because it worked. Because it taught the team to prioritize clarity over ceremony.

He kept tinkering. A little script to clean up old photos. A quick prototype for a scheduling tool. A messy but charming UI to track hikes. He joked to himself that he was on a Stage-8 Reset:

- Roadmap: one feature at a time.
- Tech: fast to build, even easier to extend when needed.
- People: a few mentees, zero org charts.
- Process: as light as breath.

In the evenings he mentored young engineers online - one in Dallas, another in São Paulo, two more he'd met through open-source channels. They asked about scaling, about fundraising, about velocity. Sam surprised himself with his answer.

"Move slower. Care deeper. The rest follows."

They wrote this down as if it were revelation. For Sam, it was simply the truth rediscovered.

Echoes From the Old World

Sometimes, messages from his old colleagues arrived like postcards from a past life.

Jonas sent a photo of the company's stock ticker mounted in their gleaming new lobby. The plaque beneath it read: Our Public Debut. Sam smiled politely at the image, though it felt as distant as a childhood memory.

Priya emailed a short note from her new nonprofit project:
"We're building tools for high-school teachers now. No investor theatrics. No runway alarms. The world is a better place again."

Amira texted a picture of her newborn daughter with the caption:
Sleep deprivation is better when it's voluntary.

Sam wrote back with warmth, but he kept the exchanges brief. Success, he had learned, was gravitational; it pulled you into its orbit until you mistook acceleration for purpose. He wasn't ready to orbit anything yet.

Then, one Friday afternoon, an unfamiliar number flashed on his screen. He answered hesitantly.

"Sam Desai," a voice sang, "guess who needs a guest judge for a hackathon?"

He blinked. Mei Chen. It had been years, but her cheerfulness was unmistakable.

"We're doing a remote-hybrid event," she said. "Students, early founders, ridiculous ideas. You'll love it."

He hesitated a moment, then laughed. "Send me the link."

That evening he set up an old webcam, adjusted the lighting, and felt an unexpected rush of excitement - an energy he hadn't felt since the early days of CareerLens.

The Return of the Pulse

The hackathon unfolded like a weekend-long heartbeat. Teams rushed between breakout rooms, demos crashed spectacularly, ideas mutated under pressure. Sam judged AI-powered climate dashboards, learning-games for kids, fintech toys held together by hope and duct tape. He loved every minute.

One team's app collapsed mid-demo. Instead of wincing, Sam laughed - not derisively, but with the affection of someone who had grown up on spectacular failures.

Failure made him alive again.

Sunday evening, Mei asked him to give closing remarks. He looked at the grid of tired, hopeful faces and spoke from instinct:

"Forget the investor deck. Build one steel thread that works - something a real person can touch and feel today."

Heads nodded on-screen.

"The rest," he added, "will come when it deserves to."

Messages poured into the chat - thank-yous, questions, appreciation. One student wrote:

"That line changed how I see my project."

The comment glowed on the screen long after he logged off.

The next morning he brewed coffee slowly, watching sunlight creep across the counter. The weekend's energy lingered like a warm hum beneath his ribs. He opened the chat transcripts, re-reading the earnest questions:

- *How do we pick a tech stack when everything changes?*
- *How do you know when to ship?*
- *What if investors don't get it?*

His answers seemed almost embarrassingly straightforward:

"Pick something you can easily delete later."
"Ship when you're proud to show your mom."
"If investors don't get it, find customers who do."

Simple truths, earned through hard miles.

Mentorship and Meaning

Over the next few weeks, several hackathon teams kept in touch. They sent him prototypes, shaky demos, screenshots riddled with bugs. He responded between hikes, in grocery store parking lots, on slow evenings with a cup of tea.

Some nights he stayed up on Discord, debugging alongside founders he had never met in person. Their energy reminded him of the early chapters of his own journey: chaotic, hopeful, unpolished.

One young founder messaged him in frustration, "We're arguing about the processes again. Should we be formalizing our workflow?"

Sam chuckled as he typed back:

"Great teams don't obsess over process. They obsess over impact. Show me how a user's life improved this week - that's the only workflow that matters."

They responded with awe, as if he had handed them a secret map. But for Sam, this was simply memory - a truth rediscovered.

That evening, after a long mentoring session, he sat outside under the fading Texas sky. The horizon glowed violet. He realized his concept of the steel thread had evolved.

It wasn't just about the thinnest working product slice anymore.
 It wasn't about velocity or demos or investor optics.

It was about the simplest, most honest connection between people and purpose.

He opened his journal and wrote:

Steel Thread = Integrity × Simplicity × Impact

He circled the word *Integrity* twice.

The Road Ahead

A few weeks later, Ava flew to Austin for a design conference. They met for lunch under a canopy of oaks. She studied him with a tilt of her head.

"You look younger," she said.

"I deleted half my calendar."

"That's way better than any Botox."

They laughed. She described her new ethics-in-AI startup, early-stage, principled, small. Then she said casually, "We could use a technical advisor. Very light-touch. You wouldn't have to wear a blazer."

Sam stirred his coffee. "I'm trying not to collect titles again."

"Then pursue meaning this time," she said. "You've always been good at that."

He promised he'd think about it.

Later that day, he found an email from Priya:
We spent a decade chasing scale. Turns out people actually crave proportion.
She attached a podcast link where she spoke with newfound clarity and calm. Sam listened during a sunset walk and felt quietly proud.

A few days after that, the young founder from the hackathon called. Her team had pivoted, found traction, even secured a small seed round.

"We need someone who's done the hard parts," she said. "Would you consider being our fractional CTO? Just a few hours a week."

Sam paused, feeling old adrenaline stir. "Maybe," he said. "Let's talk after I finish this hike."

She laughed. "Deal."

Two opportunities. One steady heart. He didn't answer either immediately. Instead, he looked over the ridge, wind brushing his hair, and savored something he hadn't tasted in years:

Possibility.

That night, his kids challenged him to a chess game.

"You used to be really good, right?" his youngest asked.

"I used to be really busy," Sam said. "That's not the same thing."

Laughter filled the living room. Later, his wife asked gently, "Do you miss it?"

"The company?" he asked.

"The rush."

He thought for a long moment. "I miss giving my everything. But I don't miss the reasons behind."

His routines soon became rituals: slow coffee, morning walks, small coding experiments without deadlines. He built a tiny open-source subtitle generator; it gained a few hundred GitHub stars and several heartfelt thank-you notes from accessibility advocates. The impact felt real, immediate, unfiltered.

He jotted ideas for his next chapter on sticky notes:
Fractional CTO practice. Mentorship platform. Micro-product lab.

The notes covered his desk like seedlings waiting for rain.

On the last day of his sabbatical, he hiked before dawn. At the overlook, the sunrise painted the hills in copper and gold. He thought of everything behind him - every launch, every layoff, every restoration and loss.

Every version of himself.

He whispered, "Thank you," not to anyone in particular, but to the thread that had held through all of it.

Then he turned toward home, ready to start another loop.

Closing Business Snapshot

Stage	Description	Notes
Transition	Post-IPO Sabbatical	No formal company Affiliation
Focus	Mentorship, open-source projects, fractional consulting	Personal experimentation Stage
Revenue	Irrelevant	"Freedom time" as Sam called it.

Concept Learned: Building an Engineering Roadmap Based on Company Vision

During his sabbatical, Sam realized something he had forgotten in the climb from Manager → Director → VP:

Most engineering roadmaps weren't connected to anything real.

They were shaped by the loudest stakeholder, the nearest fire, or the most urgent metric.

A decade of leadership had taught him something uncomfortable: Engineering roadmaps fail not because of poor planning, but because they lack a philosophy.

The great roadmaps - the ones that shaped resilient systems and healthy teams - always anchored themselves to something beyond immediate features. They translated the company's vision into a sequence of technical commitments that were coherent, humane, and survivable.

Sitting outdoors during his break - feet in river water, notebook balanced on his knee - Sam finally saw the pattern.
Every roadmap he'd built under pressure had drifted into tactical work: backlog fatigue, sales-driven features, political escalations, perfect-now-or-never deadlines.
None of them asked the first question a builder should ask:

"Where are we actually trying to go?"

He realized that the best engineering leaders didn't predict the future-they constrained it. They shaped a corridor wide enough for innovation but narrow enough for teams to stay aligned.

The roadmap was not a calendar.
It was a commitment to a direction.

A company vision wasn't a slogan; it was an architectural primitive.
It defined the edges of what engineering should build, should not build, and must never compromise on.

This was the revelation he wished he'd learned ten years earlier.

How Sam Unpacked Product Vision for Engineers

He started sketching roadmaps differently - less like Gantt charts, more like storyboards.

He anchored every quarter to three questions:
- *What part of the vision moves forward?*
- *What complexity must we retire to make that movement possible?*
- *What will users experience that shows we're on the right path?*

Instead of starting with "features," he started with behaviors:

- "Users should trust us instantly."

- "The system should recover without waking people."

- "Teams should ship without fear."

Then he worked backward into engineering initiatives - clean architecture, stability efforts, enabling tools, migrations, new capabilities - not because they felt exciting, but because they made the vision *real*.

He taught mentees that a roadmap was a translation layer between aspiration and implementation.

Vision → Strategy → Systems → Teams → Rituals → Deliverables.

Change any link, and the chain breaks.

He encouraged engineers to challenge roadmap items that lacked a vision anchor.
He redrew timelines in pencil instead of pen.

He replaced "stretch goals" with "integrity goals" - work that protected the company from invisible risks.

Most importantly, he told the hackathon teams he mentored: "Don't build what users ask for. Build what the vision requires."

For the first time in years, he felt like an engineer again - not a firefighter, not an executive - someone building toward something clearer than metrics, larger than deadlines.

And that rediscovery became the most honest roadmap he'd ever written.

Chapter 12

Epilogue - A fork in the road

The house was asleep.

Down the hall, beyond partially closed doors, Sam could hear the soft rhythm of his children breathing - small, steady reminders that time was passing even when he wasn't paying attention. The ceiling fan hummed in uneven circles overhead, a percussion line he'd stopped noticing months earlier. Outside, the cicadas droned like static, the same white noise that had once filled server rooms during overnight deployments.

Yet tonight, something in the air felt different - not louder or softer, but charged, as if the world were holding its breath.

Sam sat at his desk, the glow of his monitor cutting a perfect rectangle across the hardwood. On the screen were two emails - two offers - two futures - lit side by side like twin portals waiting for him to choose an adventure.

He leaned back, letting his body sink into the chair he had assembled during his sabbatical, the one ergonomic purchase he'd decided to splurge on. The chair fit him well. The choices on the screen did not.

The cursor blinked, patient and unjudging.

The Two Possible Doors

Offer A came from a well-known venture studio that had followed his sabbatical posts, noticed his mentoring streak, and connected dots the moment he judged that hackathon. They pitched him on a portfolio of early-stage companies - all scrappy, all ambitious, all in need of a calm, senior technical mind who could help them build early momentum without burning themselves alive.

Three to four hours a week each. Choose your clients. Say no when needed. Work from Austin. Spend evenings with your kids. Teach founders how to scale without losing their humanity.

"You'd be guiding multiple teams," the email read. "Not managing. Guiding."

He liked that word. Guiding wasn't control. It wasn't orchestration. It wasn't pressure. It was direction - gentle, deliberate, earned.

Offer B was the opposite in every dimension. A hot new GenAI startup - barely six months old, pre-product, pre-funding, pre-everything except brilliance - wanted him as a co-founder. They spoke in terms of "cognitive substrate," "adaptive intelligence," and "synthetic intuition." Their pitch deck read like a prophecy:

We are not building another AI-clone.
We are building a true partner.

The email was polite but urgent:
"We need someone who understands scale and also understands souls."

He wasn't sure souls belonged in machine learning pipelines, but he admired the ambition.

Offer A meant variety, freedom, mentorship, calm.
Offer B meant storms, reinvention, sleepless nights, and the intoxicating chaos of creation.

Both paths felt logical. Both paths were seductive.
Both paths made sense for different versions of Sam - versions that now stood in the same room, waiting for him to choose which man to become next.

The cursor blinked again. Its patience was running out.

The Shadow of the Future

He clicked to expand a stack of news alerts crowding the top corner of his screen. The headlines were familiar, almost predictable at this point:

"AGI nears threshold", say top researchers

"AI models now designing next-gen hardware"
"Is middle management obsolete?"
"The race to shape digital consciousness"

He skimmed each article, recognizing the rhetoric, recognizing the rhythm. Every technological era had its signature note. Mobile phones/apps unlocked UX nirvana. Cloud computing promised the death of hardware. DevOps promised deployments without fear. Remote work promised freedom without friction. Each delivered something brilliant and something broken.

GenAI was no different - just vaster in scope and louder in consequence.
It promised thinking machines. Feeling machines. Machines that could take instructions and return insights that felt like intuition.

He closed the news tab with a sigh. "It's never the tech," he whispered. "It's always the humans."

His reflection hovered over the darkened glass - a little older, the hair at his temples betraying a few new strands of white, but eyes steadier than they had been in years.

He didn't fear AI replacing engineers. He feared AI accelerating systems humans weren't mature enough to guide.

Leadership in the AGI era wouldn't be about control. It would be about curation. About deciding what *should* be built, not just what *could* be. It would require wisdom, not merely intelligence.

The path he chose next would determine what kind of leader he became in that brave new world.

Memory as Compass

He opened the notebook that had traveled with him through layoffs, promotions, the IPO, and the sabbatical. Its edges were soft now, corners rounded by years of being stuffed into backpacks and drawers.

He flipped to the last page he'd filled during the sabbatical - a page titled:

Steel Thread = Integrity × Simplicity × Impact

He traced the words with his finger, remembering the hike that had inspired them. The river. The cedar trees. The first morning he'd woken up without a meeting waiting for him.

Could he hold onto these principles inside an AI-native startup? Possibly.

Could he hold onto them inside a fractional practice guiding many companies at once? More likely.

He jotted a note beneath:

What does the human thread look like in an autonomous world?
Where does leadership still matter?

His mind flickered through moments like snapshots:

- Mei sketching wireframes at the first hackathon.
- Carlos celebrating the seed round like they'd already IPO'd.
- Ava explaining that designer's layer, they don't erase.
- Jack dropping sarcastic truth bombs in a room full of executives.
- Priya arguing that the product wasn't performance theater.
- Amira lecturing investors about efficiency no matter who disapproved.

And himself - standing in hallways, staring into Zoom squares, sweating in front of teams - fighting for clarity in a world drowning in narratives and metrics.

Every phase had shaped him, scarred him, softened and sharpened him.

He wasn't choosing between two jobs.
He was choosing between two kinds of futures.

The Weight of Freedom

He leaned back in his chair, letting the silence deepen.

Offer A wasn't the easy path. It was the intentional one. The calibrated one. The one built from hard-won understanding.

It was the path that let him serve many builders instead of becoming swallowed by one more machine. It let him cultivate wisdom, not just deploy expertise. It let him step into the AGI era with clear eyes, guiding the next generation of founders the way he wished someone had guided him.

He imagined his life on this path: hikes in the morning, deep work in the afternoon, mentoring calls that didn't feel like transactions. Saturday chess games with his kids. Time to think, time to teach, time to breathe.

Offer B was for the version of him who still needed to prove something. The fighter. The builder. The one who once believed that success meant ringing a bell in a stock exchange.

He made peace with that version of himself years ago. He didn't need to prove anything now. He needed to practice what he believed.

He whispered, almost amused by the clarity, "I'm not done building... but I'm done burning."

The Voice of the Past

His phone buzzed. A message from Mei.

You were amazing with those hackathon kids.
Whichever road you choose, keep that light.
The world needs fewer system builders and more courage builders.

He smiled. Mei always found the truth tucked inside the moment.

Another notification pinged - this one from Ava:
Saw a talk today on human-centered AI. Made me think of you.
Call me when you choose. I'll be proud either way.

He sat with those messages, letting the warmth of them settle into him.
Support, not pressure. Insight, not expectation.

Those were the relationships he wanted more of - relationships that moved at the speed of trust, not the speed of ambition.

Time to Make that Commitment

The rain outside thickened, tapping the window with a rhythm steady enough to feel like a drumbeat. The candle beside him flickered, casting soft shadows across the room.

He turned back to the screen.

Offer A.
Offer B.

Two futures. Only one aligned with the man he'd become.

He clicked on Offer A.
His fingers hovered over the keyboard.

He inhaled, slow and steady.

Then he typed:

I'm in.
Let's begin the next chapter.
My only condition: We build companies that stay human, no matter how intelligent the systems become.

He hit send before doubt could return.

The cursor stopped blinking. The decision was made.

A quiet confidence washed through him - not triumph, not relief, but a serene alignment between belief and action.

He had chosen the path that let him shape many, not serve one.

The World as the Oyster

He stood and walked to the window. The storm had eased; the clouds were clearing. A thin slice of moonlight spilled across the wet leaves, turning them silver.

He felt something he hadn't felt since the early days of CareerLens - possibility humming in his bones, but this time without the frantic urgency of youth.

This was "possibility with proportion".

He whispered into the quiet room, "This time, I build the way I wish we had built."

His reflection in the glass looked older, wiser, and ready - not for battle, but for stewardship.

Sam Desai had built, scaled, stumbled, recovered, and rediscovered. Now he would guide.

The future - AGI-fueled, uncertain, alive - would not wait.
But for the first time in years, he no longer felt behind.

Tomorrow, he will begin again.

Concept Learned: The Minimum Viable Future

In a world racing toward automation and artificial intelligence, Sam found himself asking quieter, heavier questions. What does it mean to build responsibly? What version of the future are we deploying, and who maintains it?

He realized that engineering's true evolution wasn't about smarter machines - it was about wiser makers. The **Minimum Viable** Future was his attempt to codify that shift. If the MVP validated what worked, the MVF validated what was *worth* working toward. It was a principle of proportional progress: build the smallest step forward that still honors humanity.

The concept wasn't abstract. It was engineering logic applied to ethics - constraints, iteration, and learning loops for civilization itself.

How Sam Embraced an Uncertain Future

He began to document his thoughts in a growing file titled The Minimum Viable Future Manifesto. It contained four succinct principles, each echoing a lesson he had learned the hard way:

- Empathy as Architecture: Systems should flex around people, not the reverse.
- Transparency as Code: Complexity without clarity is just risk disguised as progress.
- Accountability as Deployment: If you can't stand by a release, you shouldn't ship.
- Curiosity as Culture: Keep asking questions even after the system says "done."

He never published it. Not yet. Some truths need runtime before release. Instead, he refined it quietly, treating it as a staging environment between who he was and who he wanted to become.

When he finally powered down the laptop, the room fell into candlelight. Outside, the rain had turned to mist. The steel thread that began as ambition now hummed with purpose. Tomorrow would bring the next version - not of software, but of self.

Balki's Bio

Balki Kodarapu is a fractional CTO, engineering advisor, and startup builder who spent more than two decades scaling high-velocity engineering teams across fintech, health-tech, AI-native SaaS, and hyper-growth startups.

He helped organizations from 2-person founding teams to 1,000+ employee pre-IPO companies navigate the complexities of technical strategy, team culture, architecture modernization, platform rebuilds, developer experience, and the messy, human reality of leadership during hyper-scale.

Balki is the creator of *DevEx IQ*, a framework that assesses engineering excellence and organizational health; the founder and Fractional *CTO at YourCTOinUS*; and an active mentor to engineers and early-stage founders worldwide.

He writes about engineering leadership, developer experience, GenAI strategy, and humane scaling - always with one principle in mind: *technology doesn't build itself; people do.*

CTO in the Loop is his first narrative book, blending fiction with emotionally true experiences from a lifetime in the craft.

www.ingramcontent.com/pod-product-compliance
Lightning Source LLC
Chambersburg PA
CBHW061725020426
42331CB00006B/1090